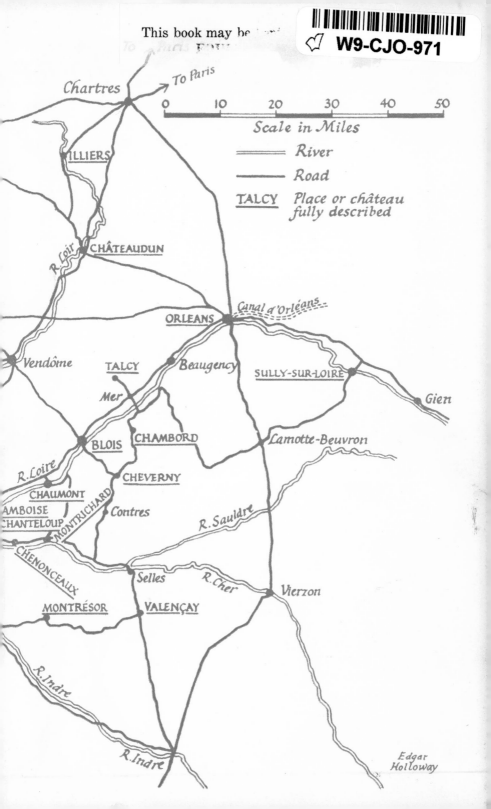

CHATEAUX OF THE LOIRE

SULLY. '. . . *there, bathed by the waters of its moats, the vast cylindrical towers of a feudal fortress stand before you.*'

CHATEAUX
OF THE LOIRE

BY

VIVIAN ROWE

38652

PUTNAM
GREAT RUSSELL STREET LONDON
1958

FIRST PUBLISHED 1954

REVISED EDITION 1958

Made and printed in Great Britain by

Hunt, Barnard & Co, Ltd, Aylesbury, Bucks

Contents

Plates

PREFACE

THE fact of the title being *Châteaux of the Loire* and not *The Châteaux of the Loire* is perhaps not sufficient in itself to stress that this book is a selection, not a complete record of all the buildings worth seeing in that part of France. The choice of those described is an entirely personal one.

The choice of historical episodes is equally personal; no single volume could describe the past associations of the châteaux in detail. For the same reasons of space many of the interesting characters of the Renaissance period have had to be omitted.

Spelling of names has presented certain difficulties. I have preferred the French form Catherine de Médicis to the Italian or Anglicised ones, partly because she was a French Queen, and partly because those who visit the châteaux will find that she is always so described by the French themselves. I have kept to the French spelling for the Kings of France, to avoid possible confusion with English sovereigns of the same name. On the other hand, to refer to Joan of Arc by any other name would be likely to shock any English-speaking reader, so I have kept the Anglicised form. Maurice of Saxony is sometimes described by his French title of Maréchal de Saxe, as both forms are current in history books.

To help the reader who may be weak on dates, I have added an appendix giving a chronological table of the Kings of France, and a list of some of the important dates in the Renaissance period and in the life of Joan of Arc.

ACKNOWLEDGMENTS

In common with many other authors of travel books concerning France, I am greatly indebted to M. Maurice Vignon for valuable help and guidance.

My thanks are due to the French Government Tourist Office in London for the loan of all the photographs which illustrate this book and to the *Geographical Magazine* for the loan of the colour process blocks used to illustrate the jacket.

THE PHANTOMS OF THE CHATEAUX

C'est vous qu'on voit errer, ô splendides maitresses,
Vous qui, dans vos tombeaux, sommeillez tout le jour,
   Diane, Marguerite, ô Reines, ô Duchesses,
   Fantômes des vieux temps et de la vieille cour.
Vous revenez la nuit; vos amants, vos poètes
Marchent à vos côtés, fiers, souriants et beaux;
   Contant de gais propos, chantant des odelettes
   Les couples enlacés glissent sous les bouleaux.

       André Theuriet

O splendid Paramours, who roam by dark
And in the day lie hidden in your tombs,
   Diana, Margaret, Duchesses, Queens,
   Dim ghosts of bygone days and Royal Courts,
The night is yours: gallants and poets walk,
Smiling and handsome, proudly at your side.
   With chatter gay and simple song, enlaced,
   Beneath the birches, phantom couples glide.

TIME AND PLACE

IT was high summer. Four of us were on our way westwards; the owner of the car in which we travelled,
a long-suffering friend who must at times have felt
as though he were acting as unpaid chauffeur; my wife,
delightfully indifferent to which road we took provided
there were good hotels and good food on the way; my
son, enjoying a last holiday before being called up for
his National Service and interested in everybody and everything; and myself, so successful a guide that everything
I wanted to see was somehow mysteriously on our route.
We had come speeding away from those white cliffs of
France that match the white cliffs of Kent; we had paid
our respects to Paris; the way to the Loire was open to us.

Far behind lay Chartres, though on this flat road the
dissimilar twin spires would long accompany us before
dissolving into the heat haze. Before and beside us, out of
sight beyond the horizon, was an expanse of ripened corn,
the 'deep ocean swell of wheat' of which the poet of
La Beauce, Péguy, writes. In the drowsiness inspired by
smooth speed in summer heat, it was easy to drift into a
daydream in which the wheat was indeed a sea gilded by a
Polynesian sun, rippling and murmuring in the wind; the
birds, emerging for a moment from out of the depths to be
silhouetted a purple-black against a cloudless sky, were
the flying fish of the tropics.

Formless and featureless as the sea itself is this strange

13

land of La Beauce. Once part of it was a great forest in which the Druids enacted those ceremonies of which so much has been written and so little is known. The cathedral of Our Lady at Chartres was itself built upon the site of one of their places of worship, which the Romans had taken over and put to their own uses. How the forest disappeared and how La Beauce got its name, is best told by Rabelais, whose country we approached.

King Grangousier decided to send his son, Gargantua, to Paris 'to know what was the study of the young men of France at that time.' A horse of more than usual strength was needed to carry Gargantua's solid weight; happily, 'in the same season Fayolles, the fourth King of Numidia, sent out of the country of Africa to Grangousier, the most hideous great mare that ever was seen . . . She was as big as six elephants.'

Thus mounted, Gargantua went on his way, accompanied by his pedagogue, his page, and his train. They 'were very pleasant till they came a little above Orleans, in which place there was a forest of five-and-thirty leagues long, and seventeen in breadth, or thereabouts. This forest was most horribly fertile and copious in dorflies, hornets and wasps . . . But Gargantua's mare did avenge herself handsomely of all the outrages therein committed upon beasts of her kind . . . For as soon as . . . the wasps had given the assault, she drew out and unsheathed her tail, and therewith skirmishing, did so sweep them, that she overthrew all the wood alongst and athwart, here and there, this way and that way, longwise and sidewise, over and under . . . in such sort that never since hath there been there, neither wood nor dorflies. Which Gargantua took pleasure to behold, and said to his company no more but this, *Je trouve beau ce*, I find this pretty; whereupon that country hath been ever since that time called Beauce.'

There are other, and perhaps more scientific, explanations

of the disappearance of the forest and of the origin of the name; not all of them make any better sense.

But the land of Rabelais and the Renaissance lay still before us, and Chartres and the Gothic world behind. For the moment we were suspended not so much in space as in time. For with the cathedral of Chartres we had turned our backs also upon the age in which it could have been created.

We are far enough away from that age now to see the events of centuries foreshortened into one dynamic movement. Through the Dark Ages the great wave of Christian belief is present, barely visible as a strong ground swell; then it rises in one of the greatest moral upsurges in all human history. Men were happy to dedicate their lives to God: their churches and cathedrals were songs of praise and gladness, reaching to the heavens. The first crusades were a harnessing of warlike spirits to the heavenly chariot. The monasteries, offering no reward for selfless devotion but in the life hereafter, spread the 'glad tidings' anew over much of the civilised world.

A wave is not timeless; it reaches its appointed crest, its moment of supreme magnificence and power, then crashes into the trough: thus did the Gothic wave. Its effects were still to be long-felt, but the power had gone from it. Man's ideals had proved beyond his capacity to maintain them. The Church became the playground of politicians; the monasteries, nurseries of luxury and houses of sloth; even the cathedrals were built to the glory of man. In Europe, the light of man's soul burned dim again.

Then, at the end of the Hundred Years War, a new spirit burst into flame, spreading into France from Italy. In France it burned most brightly in a small area along the valleys of the Loire and its tributaries which, for want of a better single word, I shall inaccurately call Touraine though it starts with the Orléannais and ends with Anjou.

The period of the greatness of Touraine begins with one woman and ends with another. The curtain rises on Joan of Arc arriving at Chinon on a cold spring day of 1429; it falls on the death-bed of Catherine de Médicis on the eve of the Epiphany, 1589. The one was a simple girl dedicated to her heavenly visions, a figure of the Gothic age born too late; the other, a symbol of her own times, remains an awful warning to all politically-minded women.

Between this rise and fall, the chivalrous male attitude towards women had disappeared; far from regretting it, women for the first time emerged as potent forces in the commonwealth. The châteaux which with the lyric poems of the times remain as the permanent record of the French Renaissance, were, in the main, built for women and often by women. Touraine became the very capital of Amazonia.

Why did this little corner of France become the theatre on which was played by turns the comedy and the tragedy of French history? Why Touraine more than Normandy, or Champagne, or Picardy, or any other part of France? There is no single answer, for history is no more than the collective life of a people, as contradictory, diverse and difficult to explain as the behaviour of any single one of its constituent individuals.

The choice of Touraine was in part a reaction against Paris. Paris, forever against the Government of the day, was a dangerous place for kings, princes, rulers and governors, blowing hot today and cold tomorrow. Catherine de Médicis complained that 'all the towns of the kingdom put together would not bring me half of the evils that I endure from Paris alone.'

Catherine was naturally a very biased witness, but the plebian and unprejudiced Dr. François Rabelais writes in much the same terms: 'all the city was risen up in sedition, they being, as you know, upon any slight occasion, so ready to uproars and insurrections, that foreign nations wonder at the patience of the Kings of France who do not by good justice restrain them from such tumultuous courses . . .'

Paris, then, was a place to which the kings would come when they had to for affairs of state. Even then, Saint Germain first, Fontainebleau later and Versailles last were often preferred, for safety's sake, to the Louvre and the Tuileries; and Fontainebleau and Versailles came into their own only after the kings of France, beginning with Henri IV, had made themselves masters of their kingdom. In earlier days some suitable provincial headquarters, where the monarchs could relax, was a necessity.

At the beginning of our period, Burgundy was an enemy (the Burgundians delivered Joan of Arc to the English), Normandy was divided between English and French, Picardy was under constant threat from the Flanders-based forces of the Empire. Touraine was an obvious choice; access to Paris was relatively easy over almost flat roads; there were innumerable lovely riparian sites for building country houses in the rich green valleys; the colourful moorlands on the watersheds provided the essential rough country for hunting; above all, the people were easy-going, cheerful, peace-loving.

Of all the peoples of France, those of Touraine are perhaps the most fundamentally French. They are essentially descendants of the original Gallic tribes; invaders of many kinds have swept over their lands, and they have absorbed them all. They have the reputation of being lazy. Balzac, one of the great sons of Touraine, sums them up cruelly in a four-line dialogue:

'Tourangeau, would you like some soup?'

'Yes.'

'Bring your bowl along.'

'I'm not hungry any more.'

This is unjust to the men of Touraine. However quickly

B

you may travel through the Touraine, you cannot but
be impressed by the hard work that has gone into vineyard and field and garden. The injustice hurts only because
it has a tiny element of truth in it; the Tourangeau works
very hard indeed, but he works in his own way and at his
own time. He is a man to whom it is only necessary to say,
'I want this done'; sooner or later, and usually not too
much later, it will be done. Stand over him, tell him where
and when and how it is to be done, and you may well wait
for ever for it. This purely passive resistance of the Loire
countryside was certainly much pleasanter to the Court than
the very active resistance of the people of Paris.

The climate, too, had much to recommend it. It may,
in the more densely afforested days, have been a little
wetter than now, when the annual rainfall averages under
26 inches, spread over 160 days. Spring comes early, sometimes too early, at the end of February; and then the countryside shines with snowdrops and violets and the blossom of
almond and apricot before the certainty of continuing
fine weather has been reached. Frosts in April, and storms
in May and June do the more damage in some years. In spite
of this, the harvest is in by the end of July, just before the
time of great heat, *les grandes chaleurs*, when the temperature
rises to 85 in the shade. In August and September the grass
dries up everywhere except upon the *prées* or water-
meadows, the streams cease to run, and the Loire becomes
so shallow that this great, broad river can almost be crossed
on foot. The vintners rub their hands with joy as the dairy
farmers grumble, for the hotter it is, the better the wine
will be. A hot September, in the local phrase, 'makes the
wine.'

During the great years, Touraine was not the 'Garden of
France' that it is now. The forests and heaths covered immense areas now under cultivation. The forests, then as
now, were of oak and hornbeam, elm and chestnut. The

very bracken of the heaths served the farmers in their efforts
to expand cultivation on to the poorer soils of the hills.
The dried bracken formed the humus that the soil needed,
usually after having served as litter for the cattle. Even
now the title of 'Garden of France' is a misnomer; many
visitors have been disappointed to find that the intense
cultivation of the rich valleys alternates with much woodland and scrubby waste which gives the 'Garden' a strangely
untidy look.

However, even in the early days of the Renaissance,
Touraine was celebrated for its fruit; Rabelais (who was a
distinguished doctor as well as humorist) praises the pears,
'juicy and of a flesh as good for the sick as for the well.'
The honey of the Gâtine was the delight of the sweet-
toothed. The delicacy of the river fish made meatless
Fridays a pleasure. The game was abundant. In fact there
was a profusion of all that was needed for the table,
including excellent wines, and Touraine acquired then a
reputation for gastronomy that lasts into our present day.

Then there was that magnificent but unhappy river, the
Loire. It is the longest river in France, fourth longest in
Western Europe, ceding third place to the romantic Tagus
by a miserable seventeen miles, a very king of rivers.

It rises far away in the south-west at Mont-Gerbier-de-
Jonc in the Cévennes, almost within sight of the Mediterranean. It passes through the Massif Central, past Le Puy,
Roanne, Nevers and Gien; it comes out through the low
hills past Orleans, Blois, Amboise, Tours, Saumur and
Nantes to the flat countryside of its mouth at Saint-Nazaire.
It waters twelve *départements*. It is fed by eight tributaries,
some of them fine rivers in their own right, three on the
right bank (Nièvre, Maine, Erdre) and five on the left bank
(Allier, Cher, Indre, Vienne and the Sèvre Nantaise). From
the map, it ought to be the major waterway of France,
whereas in fact, as you have read above, it is almost possible

to cross its great width in Touraine on foot at the height of summer.

Recently, correcting the proofs of some oddment I had written concerning Shakespeare, I found that the Loire had been so much upon my mind that I must actually have typed 'Loire' for 'Lear' (for let us be honest, most printers' errors are really authors' errors).

' For "Loire" read "Lear" '; one of those silly phrases that live in the memory and send the imagination coursing like a hare. King Loire (all 611 miles of him) betrayed by his own daughters and now living out a paralysed and useless existence. His daughters, the tributaries, do indeed betray him. Some of them flood and, as they recede, draw down vast quantities of earth which they discharge into the Loire. Slowly, with an awful inevitability, over the centuries they have choked their father, until now only the section below Nantes will carry river traffic. Where its stream was once broad, deep and unimpeded are now islands of a soil so rich that the farmers constitute a vested interest against any attempt to make the river navigable once again.

In the old days, when roads were poor and few, the Loire was a valuable means of communication and transport. The Normans were able to sail up it and attack Tours. It once had its own great equivalent of a Hanseatic Company at Tours, a rival to the river merchants of Paris who gave to the capital the ship that still dominates the city's coat of arms. The last attempt to use the upper Loire commercially was as recent as 1844.

The new steamboat was to bring back all the river's ancient glories; four navigation companies were formed to carry passengers by paddle-boat from Orleans to Nantes. There was much prejudice to be overcome; the boilers of steamboats had been bursting right and left, and the public was more inclined to watch them from a safe distance than to pay good money to embark upon them. French inventiveness is not easily baffled; the new boats incorporated safety devices (including, I believe, spring-loaded safety valves) and were proudly named the *Inexplosibles*.

Alas for the Loire, on March 26, 1846, the Duc de Nemours and the Duc de Montpensier opened up the new railway from Paris to Tours. It could not be long before the line was extended to Nantes. The steamboat, even if its journeys were not all too often interrupted by sticking fast on sand-banks, could not compete with the railway. One by one, the *Inexplosibles* and the *Paquebots* gave up, and even the ultra-modern *Etincelle* saw takings vanish to the point of total disappearance; after a thousand years, the upper Loire was left without commercial traffic.

All that, however, lay far in the future at the time of the Renaissance. Then the river was one of the greatest attractions of the Touraine: a broad silver stream beautiful to look at, and immensely practical for getting from place to place along its banks, besides providing an easy outlet to the open sea.

But for this betrayal of the Loire, Tours might well have become the capital of France. It is not easy for those who live in Great Britain, where we have so shamefully allowed our waterways to perish, to appreciate the vital importance of the water-borne traffic in earlier centuries. Even to this day, a substantial proportion of France's heavy goods is carried by water: France, far from letting the waterways decay, is developing new ones, as the hydro-electric schemes come to fruition on the river Rhône, to provide easy pas sage for barges from Marseilles to the Rhine at Strasbourg and to the Channel via the Seine. In mediæval and Renaissance times, what could not be carried by water often could not be carried at all. The river was the highroad of trade, and from the moment that navigation became even a little more dangerous on the Loire, Tours could do less and less to challenge the superiority of Paris. Geography makes history.

The Hundred Years War was over, virtually, with the burning of Joan at Rouen. Her Dauphin, her inhumanely ungrateful Dauphin, had been crowned King in 1429. There was a King of France now, no more a mere King of Bourges. Sixty years of relatively peaceful consolidation of the monarchy followed. Charles VIII, restrained and immensely strengthened by his marriage to the bourgeois-minded Anne of Brittany, became a king powerful enough to undertake a foreign war, the expedition into Italy which opened 'the first chapter in Modern History'. The King of France by then was rich enough to have an army of 30,000 men, mainly cavalry, with Swiss foot-guards and Scottish archers. He freed Pisa and entered Florence in triumph, a 'King conspicuous for his ugly face, his misshapen figure' and his dress of black velvet and cloth of gold. He came to Italy and conquered; but he also came to Italy and was conquered. To drive him from Italy needed the combination of Venice, Spain, the Pope, Milan and the Emperor. He retired with great honour; he also retired the captive of Italian artists. The ugly husk covered an artistic kernel.

As a generous patron of the arts, he brought artists of the Italian Renaissance back with him to France; to France, and above all to Touraine. France was ready for them; after centuries of spiritual starvation, the French accepted ravenously all that Italy had to offer in the arts. Under this new influence even language blossomed afresh; Touraine fashioned the French that is spoken today.

Then came the strangest episode of this giving and taking; if Italian artists captivated the King and his court, Touraine captured the artists. For whereas, let us say in Provence, they might have done no more than repeat their architectural triumphs of Italy, the landscapes and the light of Touraine caused them to create a style entirely new. It would be ridiculous to deny the obvious Italian influence of much of their work, but it would be no less ridiculous to underestimate the overwhelming influence upon them of these new conditions. Here were none of the dark blue and violet shadows of the burning Italian sun; here was no sky of deep, unbroken blue against which the brightest colours paled. Here was luminosity indeed, but gentle, not fierce; a sky blue, but blue of a most delicate shade and never without a little fleet of high, white clouds floating gracefully across it. Here the shadows were infinite variations of grey. The rivers of Touraine were not blue but silver; the background was not rugged mountain, but gently-contoured hill; no harsh bare earth, but all the imaginable range of greens of grass and trees and crops.

To those sons of Italy the new circumstances must have presented a challenge to all their preconceived ideas. What was right and fitting in Italy would be a monstrous absurdity in France. They accepted the challenge; they designed buildings that wedded happily with the landscape and climate. The buildings were not the same, because the architects had adopted a new style; this different style of building demanded a new style, also, in interior decoration. French talent was latent, but it existed. Native Frenchmen were not slow in rivalling their Italian masters. Soon the valleys of the Loire and its tributaries were as La Fontaine described them (*Le Voyage de Limousin*) : 'Smiling slopes there are on either side, fine dwellings and well-planted parks, the whole countryside abounding in green meadows, vineyards and woods; so much diversity indeed that, at first sight, it might seem another world.'

Only man was vile in this era of extraordinary artistic efflorescence. The beautiful setting of the Loire valley with its superb buildings and gardens and artistic treasures of every kind was no more than the scene of a tragi-comedy in which cruelty, treachery, jealousy, lust and murder were the dominating themes. It is difficult to awaken any sympathy for the characters who walked this stage. Perhaps we ought to feel sorry for them; they were lost souls. Although this was the age of the most violent religious strife between Christian sects, it is difficult to discover any Christian behaviour in it. The dispassionate observer will find nothing to choose between Catholic and Protestant in cruelty and intolerance. Royalty itself played fast and loose with both sides.

The intelligentsia offered no lead. Rabelais, the most forthright writer of his day, though always avowedly a devout Christian, flayed Protestant and Catholic alike, and his obvious ideal was his Abbey of Thelema with its motto 'Do as you please'. The poets were neo-pagans. *Cueillez, dès aujourd'hui, les roses de la vie*, wrote Ronsard to Hélène, 'pluck life's roses now'. There is not a religious sentiment that rings true in any of the works of the Pleiad. Clément Marot emerged from the stews of Paris to write his rhymed version of the Psalms, which Calvin had set to music, and which Court and people sang at all hours of the night and day.

By a strange fatality, as soon as a character it is possible to admire came upon the scene, the glory departed from Touraine. Henri IV could not be described as having lived a saintly life; he changed his religion according to the needs of the day, he was not averse to bloodshed in battle, he was not famed for continence, yet when the time comes for him to take upon himself the dominant rôle, the whole character of the play changes. Here, at last, was a man who thought of others and for others, who did not confuse tolerance with weakness, who killed in battle but did not murder in private, who never betrayed a friend, never took revenge upon an enemy and who, having found a master-counsellor in Sully, never imposed his own will upon his minister to the detriment of the nation. A breath of good, fresh air

blows through the history of France as Henry of Navarre
becomes King Henri IV.

He was the first of the dynasty of five monarchs cut short
by the Revolution. He became master enough of France
to dispense with the need for a Touraine to which to retire
for peace and quiet. Fontainebleau was far enough away
from Paris for hunting, and for safety; so Fontainebleau
rose and Touraine declined. After Fontainebleau, Versailles;
and with Versailles, the end of the kind of life for which
Touraine was fitted.

The decline was slow, but steady. Lights burn occasionally behind the windows of the great châteaux, but they are
quickly dimmed, and the windows are dark far more often
than they are illuminated. Like so many Castles of the
Sleeping Beauty, they are quickly surrounded by weeds
and bushes; inside they are silent and deserted.

In fact, one by one, with few exceptions, they have fallen
to the State, and for long the State was no very good guard-
ian of them. You have only to read Henry James' *A Little
Tour in France*, written but seventy years ago, to realise
how neglected many of them had become: no more than
dusty, depressing reminders of a brilliant age. Then,
almost in our own times, a complete change has come over
the scene.

It is possible to be highly critical of France for many
things, to be lost in amazement that so brilliant a people
can tolerate a system of government so astonishingly
precarious to Anglo-Saxon eyes; but no praise is too great
for the way that, during the last three generations, the
national heritage of ancient buildings has been preserved.
Beginning with Viollet-le-Duc (to whom we must forgive
much for his zeal and passionate devotion to his ideals) and
Prosper Mérimée, the Ancient Monuments Department
of the Ministry of Fine Arts has, through countless changes
of Government, through financial crises and through

three wars, continued to save, repair and reconstruct old buildings with enormous energy and success. There have been failures, naturally, but the degree of success achieved can only leave other nations, and Britain in particular, ashamed of their own shortcomings in preservation. It is, I think, a pertinent comment on the French sense of values that never once, during the most difficult days of the immediate post-war period, when whole towns were in ruins, when the housing situation was desperate, when the rebuilding of ports and factories was a primary necessity for the very life of the nation, never once did I hear a complaint from a Frenchman, not even a poor and homeless one, of scarce materials, labour and money being spent on preserving and rebuilding purely artistic treasures of no material value.

Some of the châteaux are furnished, some are empty. Too often, it seems to me, in the former, the chairs that nobody will ever sit on again, the beds that will forever remain empty, the cupboards that enclose nothing, the tables that serve no purpose, are either as uninspiring as a spare suit suspended from a hanger, or as sad as the worn toys of a dead child.

Is it better to have them empty, echoing to the voice of guide and footsteps of visitors or, like Versailles, filled with roped-off furniture? I find Versailles infinitely more desolate in its furnished splendour than the emptiest of the Loire châteaux.

Who would not prefer the empty château to be filled by one's own imagination, with all the colour and animation of the most brilliant, the most animated period of French history?

CHAPTER I

Towards the Loire

(ILLIERS AND CHÂTEAUDUN)

O U R route could easily have passed through Illiers
that we did not go there was my fault. This was
an error of judgment I would not wish any reader
to make in the course of a similar journey, for Illiers is
doubtless the most charming by far of all the villages of
La Beauce.

From the banks of the Loir (to the confusion of foreigners,
le Loir is a tributary of La Sarthe, which joins with La
Mayenne to form La Maine, a tributary in its turn of
La Loire), the fourteenth-century church thrusts up above
the intervening trees and houses, and its image shivers on
the barely moving water; the sharp angles of its solid square
tower and too suddenly reduced octagonal spire soften as
under an impressionist's brush. But why should I describe
Illiers to you, when it has already been done so much better?

'Combray . . . was seen to be keeping the grey and woolly
backs of the packed houses as near as possible to its long
black cloak, as a shepherd in the open countryside does
his ewes as a protection against the wind; houses that the
remains of mediæval ramparts partly ringed here and there
with a boundary as perfectly circular as that of a little town
in a primitive painting.'

Combray? What has Combray to do with Illiers? Everything, for Illiers was, and Illiers is, 'Combray'. It was the

27

birth-place of Adrien, the father of Marcel Proust; the latter's sister, the 'Aunt Léonie' who figures so largely in the early part of Proust's great work, lived in quiet retirement at Illiers, where the sensitive adolescent Marcel came each year to spend his holidays. There her husband, 'Uncle Amiot', created a magnificent water-garden, described in vivid detail in *Swann's Way*, the first 150 pages of which are very largely descriptions of Illiers and La Beauce.

Would one dare today to buy and eat a madeleine in Illiers? It would surely prove a disappointment, could hardly hold the magic of that broken morsel 'which my Aunt Léonie used to offer me when I went to her room to bid her good day on a Sunday morning at Combray, after having steeped it in her decoction of tea or lime flowers . . .'

The genius of Proust did so much more than triumphantly recapture his 'Time Mislaid'; it awakened memories in his readers, so that today for many of them it is sufficient just to write his name to be momentarily returned to a past that otherwise would remain deep buried. All who love his work find in the development of his theme some aspect of their own youth.

Illiers can have changed but very little since Proust's boyhood, yet if you are not seeing it with his eyes you will find in it no more than a sleepy village, a tall church and old grey houses, by the side of a river that hardly flows enough in summer to disturb the water-lilies.

On this occasion, then, we did not go to Illiers; yet Marcel Proust went part of the way with me as I amused myself with thoughts of the kind of social history he might have written if his time had been a few centuries earlier, and his connection with the all-powerful Cardinals and Dukes of the Guise family. It is not difficult to imagine him watching them from afar in his youth, overwhelmed by their grandeur, being accepted by them; then year by year discovering their secrets, the moral defects behind their splendour, and giving to their final fall a dispassionate pathos. Only the French language of the time was not yet, perhaps, the instrument to achieve such a purpose.

Almost before we were aware of it, we had reached Châteaudun direct from Chartres, which is the wrong road scenically. The only proper way to approach it is from Illiers or Nogent-le-Rotrou; this road brings you to a bridge across the Loir, defended by as formidable a fortress as you will see anywhere. It gives an impression of extraordinary height for a feudal building; not until you approach quite close to it, does it become apparent that the impression is a false one and that the lower part is no more than sturdy masonry, enabling the whole construction to project from the hillside on which it is built so that the river itself serves as a moat defensive. From afar, it looks comparable with the magnificent west wall of the Mont-Saint-Michel. Inspection from nearer at hand shows the comparison to be unjustified, yet the castle of Châteaudun must be considered as one of the finest examples of a feudal fortress in France.

This is not at all the way it will strike you if you arrive, as we did, direct from Chartres. It is even a little difficult to find, as you drive through a tiny congested town still living, as it were, in the afterglow of its own sunset. All through the Middle Ages, right up into modern times, Châteaudun was a prosperous town, often needing its strong castle to defend it from jealous and less favoured neighbours. Châteaudun was the market for much of the grain of La Beauce.

On Thursdays, from immemorial custom, the farmers came in to sell their crops on samples. All through the day they haggled with the wealthy grain merchants, until the clasp of hands and the glasses of wine sealed the bargain. The further away the harvest, the lower the price, for then the merchant bore the risk of the dreaded summer thunderstorms or even more dreaded drought. After the harvest, the grain merchant sold in his turn to the miller. At every transaction, a little of the money stuck to the fingers of the good people of Châteaudun, and they prospered. Indeed, they prospered so much that it was an enviable thing to be a grain porter. Not everybody was allowed to join the Corporation of Porters; the entrance fee was as much as £40 or £50, an immense sum for working people of the nineteenth century.

His fee paid, the new member must attend his baptism. A full bottle of wine was poured over his head and he was given his nickname, the only name by which he would be known thereafter on the records of the corporation. Odd names many of them were: 'Soup-downer', 'Softy-boots', 'Butter-wallower', 'Lazy-walker'.

Henry of Navarre, who wished to see a chicken in every Frenchman's pot, would have been satisfied with Châteaudun in those days. The grain dealers sold by measure, not by weight, and as it was continually being handled, and as the grain spilled over from the bushels at each handling, the children of the town would run forward with their little bowls to scoop up all that had fallen, and hasten home with it for mother to feed to the chickens.

The railway marked the end of Châteaudun's glory, the opening in 1846, of the main line from Orleans to Le Mans, 80 miles away across the plain, ignoring this market town's importance. It survived for long as a local market, but the last straw, as its people will sadly tell you, was the wartime institution of the Office du Blé, the government's centralised grain buying agency which still prevents all private dealing. Shaking their heads, they go on to assure you that their town is dead and finished. We had reason to think otherwise, or at least to find it remarkably active for a corpse.

It had been given up as dead and finished three times before. The inhabitants of Blois and Tours joined together to burn it in 1570. It had just been resurrected when the League burned it in 1590. The next time it burned down, in 1723, the cause was quite accidental, but the effect just as devastating.

After this third conflagration, it was entirely built anew to plans by Mansart-Hardouin, and stood for a slightly longer time before the next calamity. In October, 1870, it was besieged by some 10,000 Germans. For nine hours it was gallantly defended 'by less than a thousand National Guards and their civilian supporters.' (The number of Germans tends to increase slightly, and the number of French to diminish, with the years; a nearly contemporary account puts the number of defenders at 4,000, but there is no doubt about their inferiority in arms and men or the extreme heroism of their defence). When the Germans had taken it, they burned it once again.

What remains as the bitterest memory of this wicked episode is that German officers ordered and ate a fine meal at an inn, and then set fire to it by way of grace after their meal. So nobody in Châteaudun felt that the Germans had changed much for the worse when, in 1940, they showered fire-bombs, all too successfully, on the fine old twelfth-century church of the Madeleine.

Today Châteaudun has a few old houses which managed to escape all these holocausts, a few remains of the Mansart-Hardouin plan, and a majority of streets of the anonymous kind you will find all over France in provincial towns, the insipid work of the nineteenth century.

One of these unremarkable streets leads you from the main road from Chartres to a little square deep in the shadow of great plane trees. Half-seen through the foliage is an immense twelfth-century round tower with a blue-grey conical roof. It dwarfs the two storeys of a graceful Renaissance wing of which a glimpse can be caught through a pair of iron gates. This is the château.

At this point you are eighty or ninety feet above the level of the Loir, which explains the formidable masonry so impressive from the river. The appearance of the château from the higher level is, by comparison, almost ludicrously domestic. Except for the great round tower it is no longer a powerful fortress but a pleasing dwelling-place, even in its Gothic parts. It is, in fact, remarkably interesting and almost unique in presenting the interim period of architecture between feudal strength and Renaissance grace. Why it is not better known, I shall never understand.

According to an inscription over the door, the huge cylindrical keep, over one hundred feet high without its roof, is attributed to Thibaut the Trickster, who died in 978. He must have been a trickster to some purpose, enjoying a macabre little joke by erecting it, doubtless on Walpurgis' Night, a good century after his death. Whoever built it, it is a superb twelfth-century keep, over 50 feet in diameter, with tapering walls more than 13 feet thick at the bottom. The top of the conical roof is more than 150 feet high; it is worth the climb (at least to the young and energetic) to see the magnificent fifteenth-century wheel rafterwork supporting the pepper-pot roof.

Joining the keep to the west wing is the flamboyant *Sainte Chapelle*, finished just before its founder died in 1468. Here, in his own chapel, Dunois came often to pray. History, which has recorded the last period of Joan of Arc's life in minute detail, falls silent on the thoughts of the other characters in her drama after her death. We are left without an answer to the one question which would decide what manner of man this Dunois really was; is it possible that her bluff, hearty, honest supporter and protector, her brother-in-arms, made no effort to save her? There is no record that he did.

Did then the much-praised Bastard of Orleans only use her to help win his war? Did he, after all, ever believe in

1. CHATEAUDUN. 'The north wing is pure Renaissance, ending in an open-work staircase of honour, a rather poor relation of the glorious ones which were to follow.'

2. SULLY. *As Joan of Arc left on her last and fatal journey, 'Sully's strong white towers diminished and disappeared behind her.'*

her voices and her visions? Strange, is it not, that so gallant a figure should for a time disappear from sight until well after her death, once her capture had proved the spell Joan cast around herself to be unavailing?

In this, his own chapel, the visitor cannot but wonder in what terms he made his peace with God. He lived on, successful in war and prosperous in peace, except for a momentary fall from regal grace which can have troubled him but little, for nearly forty years after Joan's ashes had been scattered on the waters of the Seine. If ever he thought of her, this surely must have been the place. Yet, with one possible exception, such thoughts were not made manifest in this chapel.

Perhaps, after all, his conscience was tranquil; perhaps he had done all that he could to save her, and that history has not recorded it. The enigma can hardly now be solved.

Can any hint be found in the life-size statue of Saint Catherine, which, with those of Saint Elizabeth of Hungary, Saint Apollinaria and Saint Barbara, he decorated his chapel? It is all very vague; Saint Catherine is no more prominent than the others of these splendid specimens of early Renaissance statuary. It is true that Saint Catherine was Joan of Arc's very personal Saint, but then so she was of Dunois himself; it was one of the things that drew them together. If it was a gesture to her memory, it was a modest one.

In spite of the effect of tremendous height that the château gives from river level, the living quarters consist but of two floors and a steep roof above ground. The west wing was Dunois' own, begun in his time and completed in his son's. From its windows you look down on to a terraced garden, thirty feet below, itself standing high above a lateral valley and supported by enormous walls. In the north-west corner is an intricate Gothic staircase, with neat recesses in the corners that once held lanterns to illuminate

it; from the corner wing you look straight down the recti-
linear buttresses to the river more than a hundred feet
below.

The effect is amazing, and once again comparison with the
Mont-Saint-Michel is inevitable. The buttresses stretch away
before you, the foreshortening of perspective adding to
their bulk. There they have stood for centuries, there
obviously they will continue to stand (atom bombs permitting) for centuries yet to come, their strength a hearty
slap in the face of Time itself.

The north wing is pure Renaissance, ending with an
open-work 'staircase of honour', a rather poor relation of
the glorious ones to follow. The staircase in these buildings
was something much more than a means of communication
between floors. It served as a grandstand when there was a
fête in the courtyard, as a balcony from which the ladies
could watch in safety the men tilting against the popinjay
or engaging in an archery competition. It had its decorative
uses also; on it stood the richly dressed men-at-arms when
some distinguished guest was being received, the rich
colours of their uniforms setting off the beauty of carvings
and arabesques on the staircase cage.

It is most interesting to observe the two styles coming
together in this château. The Gothic curve in the earlier
chimney-pieces already developing into flamboyance, and
the flamboyance transmuted in the Renaissance into new
and richer and softer pattern. And where better should it
be seen than in Dunois' own château? Châteaudun was his
stronghold, the centre of resistance to the English against
whom, practically single-handed, he waged a life-long
war. Before he died, his work was accomplished. With
Joan of Arc he won his first successes. Year by year, battle
by battle, the home of the nobleman needed less and less
to be a fortress. Almost alone Dunois brought to France
an era of comparative peace and made possible the Renais-

sance that finds its early flowering in the wing his successors added to his château. Thanks to Dunois it could safely become a dwelling-place unfortified.

It is largely due to the extensive restoration of recent years, carried out by the *Monuments Historiques* with the most praiseworthy care and with perfect taste, that we can enjoy visiting Châteaudun today.

It is one thing to get into the town of Châteaudun; it was quite another, we found, to get out of it, at least on market day. Following a sign nicely combining the terse and the vague, *toutes directions*, 'all directions', we found the way blocked by a street market giving the lie direct to the story of Châteaudun being a dead town. It would hardly have been possible to crowd more stalls, sales vans, piles of goods, buyers and sellers than we saw there into even the large area of the square. Hurriedly we turned to the first road on the right, got lost in little streets, turned in towards our *toutes directions* road, and found ourselves inextricably involved in the market. With immense good nature, a great deal of chaff, much blowing of horns and scattering of pedestrian traffic, one or two sales vans moved over a little and enabled us to worm our way out, foot by foot. A dead town, indeed! Nowhere else, in the course of a long journey, did we find so much concentrated life. To what other parts our *toutes directions* road led, we never discovered. Still perspiring, we thankfully pursued our own way, and cared not what happened to Jack.

CHAPTER II

The Loire and Saint Joan

(ORLEANS)

THE road towards the Loire strikes straight from village to village across the plateau of La Beauce; some of the hamlets look enchanting with a tiny Renaissance château, more or less in ruins, a tiny Romanesque church and, certainly, more than one inn in which to taste a bottle of the white wine of the *Côteaux du Loir*, verging on the sweet, full-flavoured, and nectar to those who admit to enjoying wine that does not necessarily bear a snob-value label. Like all these local wines, it is a little uncertain; in the main, the vineyards are very small. The owner may make no more wine in a year than will meet the needs of his family and supply, perhaps, a single outlet, shop or restaurant or hotel; and you will seldom find the wine from any given vineyard in any other place. This adds a certain not displeasing uncertainty to one's wine drinking; there is always the chance, in some unexpected corner, of coming across a particular 'little' wine so much better than the run of the others that it lingers in the memory. Vintage wines and a limited travel allowance do not work well in harness; fortunately, in this happy land there is a different local wine to be tasted every few miles of your journey, and even the great years (as far as the term can be applied to 'little' wines) 1942, 1943, 1945, 1947, are within the purse of most travellers. Even the least distinguished of them, in the phrase of the wine-growers themselves, 'let themselves be drunk'.

Much of my life has been spent regretting the lack of time to stop at villages which, from the highroad, look so attractive. Only the cyclist really has that opportunity, and I am far from certain that they ever do. I am quite sure, though, that the French motorist does not. The immense network of French roads seems covered by miniature cars, all travelling at improbably high speeds for astronomical distances. They dart here and there like angry bees, resting only for the almost sacred hours of lunch and dinner. At all other times of the day and at most times of the night they buzz along as if the entire population of France were swarming.

Ask any garage owner, as I did, why the French have changed-over since the war to such very small cars, and you are sure to receive the answer, with a sly smile, *signes extérieurs de richesse*, those external signs of wealth by which the French tax-inspector can assess at an arbitrary figure the income of any citizen he suspects of not having declared his full revenue. The onus of proving that the income thus assessed exceeds the real one is on the taxpayer.

The very high cost of motor fuel also accounts for it in part, but I believe the main reason is purely psychological. Driving a big car has become too easy; there is no more satisfaction in driving something that practically drives itself than in shooting a sitting bird. Where cars are concerned, the Frenchman (for remarkably few women drive in France) is always *très sport*. He derives enormous satisfaction from pushing some very small car along at some practically impossible number of miles per hour. Anybody can put up an average like that with a Rolls-Royce, but only a Frenchman can do it with three or four horse-power to play with. And, after all, even the smallest car can be equipped with the loudest horns.

Orleans, which most of these toy-sized cars will have reached before us, is disappointing. There are no views of the broad Loire as you approach; you must traverse almost all the old town on the north bank before you make its first acquaintance. The suburbs seem interminable, and you have to cross a whole sad quarter destroyed partly in 1940 and partly in 1944.

In 1940, Orleans lost its centre, and with it the church of Saint Paul, a jewel of the last days of Gothic greatness; the Historical Museum, housed in a beautiful Renaissance mansion; the Joan of Arc Museum, and many other interesting old buildings. In 1943, American bombers attacked the station, returning a year later to demolish the Aubrais station and laying flat some forty acres around it in the process. In August the town was liberated, but only after an amount of destruction that will take many years yet to make good.

Orleans, in spite of damage, is the kind of place always described as 'a fine city'. It has wide boulevards, some good buildings, and a long river frontage to bear out the description; yet it remains colourless. Here one realises that, unlike most of the French provinces, the Loire valley never developed a characteristic architecture for its smaller buildings. All the creative genius of its builders went into the châteaux; there was nothing left over for the humbler people.

From the centre of the great bridge, the Pont Georges V, there is a fine sweeping view northwards, the foreground dominated by the four churches of Saint-Aignan, Saint-Pierre, Saint-Donatien and Notre-Dame-de-la-Recouvrance, and the middle distance by the Cathedral of the Holy Cross, unique in being a Gothic cathedral built out of its time in the seventeenth and eighteenth centuries, the first step on the downward path towards the full horrors of the Victorian Gothic revival. Towards the right, the Canal d'Orléans merges with the Loire and accounts for the not

inconsiderable trade on the broad quays. Corn from La
Beauce; honey from the Gâtine, famous for a thousand
years; game from the Sologne moorlands; wine from the
entire Loire valley; fruit and flowers and vegetables, leave
from here for the interior.

In spite of this present-day activity, for most of us
Orleans lives in its past; all that remains of the time of the
Maid is within a hundred yards of the modern bridge, a few
grey stones just upstream on the south bank that are the
last traces of the fort which was the scene of Joan of Arc's
first triumph. A quarter of a mile or so farther up is the
point where, on her first arrival, she was infuriated to find
herself on the wrong bank of the river. On the north side
of the river the ancient ramparts of the town as Joan knew
it are defined by the broad boulevards. Everything of hers
has gone, even the very islands in the river: the Ile Saint-
Antoine, the western end of which reached to where the
Pont Georges V now spans the river and without which,
as an anchorage for the two bridges which joined right
bank to left, the Loire could hardly have been spanned in
those days; the Grande Ile aux Boeufs, or Ile Saint-Loup,
farther to the east; the Ile Charlemagne to the west.
Nothing of Joan's is left, except a few grey stones to mark
the south end of the English-held bridge; yet she is as present
always as if no change had ever come to the town.

The siege had begun in October, 1428. Dunois flung
himself into the town, which had some twenty-five to
thirty thousand inhabitants with perhaps some five to six
thousand fighting men, rightly convinced that the Governor,
Gaucourt, would not do much good by himself. The English
army could hardly have exceeded ten thousand men, quite
insufficient to invest the town completely. Bedford did his
best with covering forts to prevent the arrival of supplies
and reinforcements, but there were gaping holes in his
envelopment, particularly eastwards.

The siege proceeded with the usual politenesses on both sides. On Christmas Day a truce was arranged from nine in the morning to three in the afternoon. To while away these unaccustomed hours of peace, Bedford felt the need of music. The Bastard kindly lent him an orchestra 'of skilled fiddlers, trumpet and clarion players, who made him great melody for several hours'. Bedford sent the Bastard a present of fresh figs, quite out of season and obtained heaven knows how. In a more practical spirit, Dunois returned a warm fur coat. At three o'clock, the stone cannon balls were again being thrown with more noise than accuracy by the cannon of both sides.

The firing of a gun was no easy matter. The stones for the French *Rifflard*, the wonder cannon of its day, weighed 120 lb. The rival English cannon would fire a stone a yard in diameter. The great art was to roll the stone down the barrel without allowing it to explode the gunpowder prematurely by impact.

Without any material change in circumstances, siege and defence continued until the spring of 1429, when rumours reached Dunois of a girl from distant Lorraine who was coming to drive the English away and to ensure the King's crowning at Rheims. Intrigued, the Bastard sent two of his gentlemen to Blois to enquire further about her. They were a little premature and had to wait a week for her arrival. Whatever report they brought back after her interview with the Dauphin, they satisfied the Bastard on one point; Joan was going to be useful to him in his fight against the English.

Towards the beginning of March, Joan sent Bedford a first letter, telling him to go home or it would be the worse for him. It is doubtful if anybody took the trouble to ensure that it reached him. Then, after maddening delays and indecision, Joan left Blois for Orleans on April 25. With her went reinforcements to the number of some three or four thousand horsemen and men-at-arms, with a large number of provision carts and four hundred head of cattle. She had achieved one ambition, to be on her way to succour the Bastard, but failed in another. She was given no authority; that was vested in Marshal Saint-Sévère, Marshal de Rais (Gilles de Rais, the 'Bluebeard' of infamous memory in the nursery) and Admiral Louis de Culen, which seems a lot of commanders for a small force. Worse still, not one of them had the least faith in her mission, but did all they could to discourage and mislead her.

The pace of the cattle set the speed of the march. They arrived at the Loire, just upstream from Orleans, on April 28. Joan, with anger flaming, discovered that she had been brought to the wrong side of the river. There must have been some reason for this decision which, in the light of subsequent events, can be seen to have been a wrong one, but Joan was not told what it was.

The approach of the reinforcements had been observed by the garrison. In the pouring rain, Dunois took boat out of range of the English arms and crossed to meet her. If his two gentlemen had given him to expect a gentle, mild-mannered young girl he must have been no little surprised. The short, broad-built country lass with the husky voice (it was curiously described as *assez voix de femme*, 'a fairly feminine voice') greeted him with no deference and little courtesy; she had been, she claimed, grossly deceived. Dunois, even if he were no more than the gruff soldier he has since been portrayed as being, had had a courtly upbringing. With considerable tact he both pacified Joan and worked out with the three commanders a practical scheme for the relief of the garrison.

His first idea was to borrow boats and send them five miles upstream to Chécy, where they would wait to ferry across the cattle and provisions which would reach there by road. Once across the river, they could proceed to Orleans by the road on the right bank, past the English-held Bastille Saint-Loup, which the garrison would undertake to mask. On inspecting the reinforcements, he decided that they were insufficient in number to run the risk of being cut off by a sortie in strength by the English, and in any case the wind was blowing downstream, in the wrong direction for this manoeuvre. Angrily Joan told him to wait a little while and all would be well. Surely enough, presently the wind backed.

In spite of this, Dunois did not feel justified in taking the risk. With infinite difficulty, and then only by promising to accompany her himself, he persuaded Joan to turn east-wards to Chécy, where she spent the night. The rest of the reinforcements were sent back to Blois to make up addi-tional strength; from there they would return to Orleans along the north bank of the river, the route that Joan had rightly held from the beginning to be the proper one. In fact it was so clearly so that one wonders if the decision to come to the left bank were not taken solely because the commanders could not bear to agree with her on any military matter.

The next day Joan and Dunois left Chécy (or, more probably, the now non-existent Château de Reuilly) for Orleans. They arrived at the Porte de Bourgogne, now marked by a railway bridge, and advanced along the length of the present Rue de Bourgogne. It was eight o'clock at night when Joan 'armed at all points and mounted on a white charger' entered in. Before her was carried her standard, also white, portraying two angels holding fleurs-de-lys in their hands, 'and a panel painted like the Annunciation' (in fact it was the image of Our Lady, having before her an angel who is presenting her with a lily).

'Thus she entered into Orleans, having the Bastard of Orleans on her left hand, armed and richly mounted. After her came many other nobles, captains and men-at-

arms, without any of the garrison, and also the townspeople of Orleans who had gone before to greet her.
As she entered, many other men-at-arms and men and
women of the town came towards her, carrying great
numbers of torches, and joyful as if they saw God Himself
descend amongst them,' according to Quicherat's collection
of the almost contemporary evidence.

As they pressed round her, the torches set fire to her
banner, which she took and whirled round her head until
the fire was extinguished. Ever increasing crowds escorted
her from the Porte de Bourgogne in the east to her lodging
near the Porte Regnart in the west, where she was received
by Jacques Boucher, treasurer to the Duke of Orleans, and
put to bed with Charlotte, his nine-year-old daughter.
Presumably to protect her virginity from the tongue of
scandal, poor Joan was seldom allowed to sleep alone.

The next day, the last day of April, brought Joan into
bitter argument with Dunois. She demanded an immediate
attack on the English. He insisted on going to Blois to
speed up the reinforcements for the attack. Baulked in this
direction, Joan relieved her feelings by sending an ultima-
tum to Bedford to clear out. Her heralds had some difficulty
in escaping alive from the English, and returned with the
answer that she should go home and mind the cows,
otherwise she would be caught and burnt. Furiously
angry at this message and the treatment of her heralds,
Joan went herself to the bridge and, in considerable danger
of capture, stood and shouted a message to Sir William
Glasdale at Les Tourelles to give up and save his life. This
was greeted by the English soldiers with cat-calls and cries
of 'cow girl', but no effort was made to take her.

The first day of May brought her nearer to the action
she desired; the Bastard, irrevocable in his decision to
leave for Blois, departed early in the morning. Joan and
La Hire went out to cover his march, but there was no

fighting. When she returned to her lodging, the people broke down the door in their anxiety to see her, so she went out and about the town on horseback. 'She carried herself so magnificently in every way as a man-at-arms might have done who had followed the war since his youth.' Tiring of this, Joan went again to harangue the enemy who, with the characteristic irreverence of English soldiers, greeted her with laughter and mockery. Next day was a day of waiting, with inspection of the English defences to pass the time. The feeling of expectation rose higher on May 3, when the garrisons of Gien, Montargis, Château-Reynard and Châteaudun began to arrive to reinforce Orleans; and in the evening, news came from Blois that another army had set out from there and was taking the northern road by La Beauce.

Dawn of the first day of action, May 4, saw Joan riding out 'with banner unfurled' at the head of five hundred men to meet the army from Blois; she was joined by the Bastard, who had already returned. Between six and seven in the morning, the head of the relieving column entered Orleans. After dinner, which was a midday meal, the Bastard told her that he had received news that Sir John Fastolfe was on his way with reinforcements for the English. Sleepy after too early a start to the day (with a heavy meal possibly contributing), Joan retired to rest, after Dunois had promised to keep her informed of developments. Sleeping, she dreamed, and awoke in agitation, crying out aloud, '*En Nom Dieu*, my counsel has told me to go out against the English, but I do not know whether it is against the forts or against Fastolfe.' She went out into the streets; the distant sound of battle could just be heard. Townspeople came to her with the rumour that, in spite of Dunois' promise, the French were attacking the Bastille Saint-Loup, and suffering heavy casualties.

Joan, once again in a tearing temper, rode out through

the Porte de Bourgogne towards the fort of Saint Loup, the only one the English held to the west of the town on the right bank, to find that Gaucourt, the Governor of Orleans and her open enemy in the Council of the Captains, had attacked and was being repulsed. As Joan advanced with her banner, the French shouted in triumph and, plucking up courage, advanced on the fort and carried it in one irresistible movement. The English retired, leaving behind them 114 dead and 40 prisoners. The French burnt and demolished the fort. On the far side of the town to the west, Talbot attempted a sortie from the Bastille Saint-Pouair, but withdrew on meeting with a larger French force.

The day had ended with the first French triumph for many months. The church bells were rung to celebrate the victory as the captains went to give solemn thanks, but to the ordinary soldiers and the people of the town, the victory was not due to the captains but to Joan. On this day the *mystique* of Joan of Arc took form.

This attack was not followed up the next day. It would seem that the impatient Joan insisted that the Bastille of Saint-Jean-le-Blanc should be assaulted, and this the Council of the Captains (perhaps because it was Joan's suggestion) refused. Making the best of a bad job, Joan decreed that, as it was Ascension Day, there should be no fighting at all. She herself went to Confession, and issued orders that no one would be permitted to take part in the great attack on the English, promised for the following day, unless he had previously confessed his sins, and unless all women of ill-repute were dismissed from the army. The churches were filled with unaccustomed penitents. The women of ill-repute went into hiding.

Whilst Joan was making these Christian arrangements, the commanders were making their own warlike ones. They decided to attack, not Saint-Jean on the south side of the river, but Saint-Laurent on the north bank, to the west. Joan had to brave them in their Council Chamber and demand to be taken into their confidence, before they would tell her. Immediately, she sent another of her forthright letters to the English, 'abandon your forts . . . go back where you belong . . . I am writing to you for the third and last time. I shall write no more.' The message was thrown to the English soldiers, whose shouted comment as they picked it up was, 'Ah! news from the harlot of the Armagnacs,' whereupon Joan retired in floods of tears.

On May 6, the French, by means of a bridge of boats, crossed to the south bank and drove the English outposts into the shelter of the Augustine convent at the end of the permanent bridge. A French attack on this was repulsed, and, as they retired to their bridge of boats, a counter-attack by the English threatened to overwhelm them. The hurried French retreat at first caught Joan up with it, but disengaging herself she called upon the men to re-form and led them in an attack which drove the English first into the convent, and then beyond it on to the bridge and to the safety of the Tourelles fort which protected the southern end.

Joan's success this day gave no more satisfaction to the Council than the previous day had done. At supper time, they sent her word that no further attack would be made until new reinforcements arrived from Blois. Joan, now stronger than ever in the support, almost the adoration, of soldiers and townspeople, refused to accept this decision. Her plan was to feint against Les Tourelles at the southern end of the bridge, and to bring the main attack to bear on Saint-Antoine at the northern end, before the English had had time to recover. As she went to leave by the Porte de Bourgogne to rejoin the troops camped ready for the attack on Les Tourelles, she met the first physical opposition.

Gaucourt rode up to the gate and barred her way. The irate people of Orleans swept him aside, and Joan passed through amidst their cheers.

The last act of the drama took place on May 7, 'the day of the Tourelles'. A bombardment by the heavy cannon across the Loire was followed by a lighter one from the culverines, transportable cannon, brought across the river and making their first appearance in history at Orleans. Then the French began their assault. To encourage them, Joan leaped down into the moat and helped to put up a scaling ladder. An arrow pierced the top part of her shoulder and came through 'six inches beyond her neck'. She cried out, and fell backwards. The English shouted 'the witch is dead', and danced for joy on the battlements.

Joan's followers carried her off; at a safe distance from the fort, with remarkable courage, she herself withdrew the arrow, crying out with pain. Suddenly she relaxed and complained no more; her saints had appeared to her, and given her ease. The wound was protected by a 'compress of lard and olive oil', and she went forward again.

Looking out from their fort, the English were first astounded, then terrified, to see their dead 'witch' advancing again to the attack, her standard ruffling in the wind. Seized by panic, they retired from the outworks to the almost impregnable inner fort.

Meanwhile, from the Orleans side, the attack on Saint Antoine had been equally successful. Caught between two fires, the English capitulated; two hundred of them were made prisoner, three hundred killed or drowned.

The next day the siege was lifted. The English were now outnumbered, they had lost control of the river and of the eastern approaches to the town. They evacuated the remaining forts, with what was left of their provisions.

Joan returned to Orleans amidst such acclamation as has perhaps never been heard there since.

From the Pont Georges V the whole of the scene of these ten days lies around you, ten of the most important days in the history of France and of England. The *mystique* of Joan of Arc gave the French the moral uplift that was needed to continue to a successful end their campaigns against the English. The relative peace that followed brought forth the Renaissance in France.

A detached view of the military operations gives food for thought. Joan arrived to find an army, small and discouraged by lack of success. She rebuilt its morale. Reinforcements flowed in, until it was no longer inferior in strength to its opponent. She led it to victory, in spite of the forebodings of some of the military experts.

Replace 'she' by 'he', and you may wonder if perhaps one day we shall have a Saint Bernard of Alamein; for if her canonisation was not due to her success at Orleans, it is difficult to see what other reason there was for it. She performed no miracles. The account of her sending a letter to Sainte-Catherine-de-Fierbois to look behind the altar for the sword which, according to legend, was used by Charles Martel at Poitiers in 732, and the successful discovery of it there, would be much nearer miraculous if it were not known that she had, herself, visited the church as recently as the previous March 4 and 5. The inference that one of the priests knew of its existence and told her of it is overwhelmingly strong; she makes no claim in her letter to divine guidance. For the rest, she was a good and kind-hearted young girl who was firmly convinced she had visions, in which she implicitly believed. There have been many other such girls who have not yet been canonised.

Whether or not emotion is the reason why she is now Saint Joan, she remains one of the most fascinating characters in all history, impossible for the average person to understand because of the great simplicity of her mind.

3. BLOIS. *The staircase 'has an octagonal container . . . the stairs and balus-trade making, in effect, a sloping bridge from pillar to pillar'.*

4. CHAUMONT. 'You enter Chaumont in the south-east corner, between two of its grand towers, over a drawbridge.'

Many years were to pass before a personality so appealing and so upright would appear again in France. She illuminates her age with a pure white light which throws the whole of the ensuing Renaissance period in France into a patchwork of shadows.

CHAPTER III

The Saint, the Statesman
and the Satirist

(SULLY)

SULLY stands on the Loire, some twenty-five miles upstream from Orleans and the farthest point eastwards of our present journeyings. Saint-Benoît, on the way, is probably the finest Romanesque building in France (Saint Benedict, the founder of the Benedictine Order, now lies buried there), but it belongs to another period altogether; its greatness had already waned before ever Joan of Arc reached the Loire.

The approach to Sully is superb; a turn off the main road, a long bridge across the river and there, bathed by the flowing, stream-fed waters of its moats, the vast cylindrical towers of a feudal fortress stand before you. This, the north side (for Sully is on the south bank of the Loire) is the mediæval castle almost exactly as Joan of Arc must have seen it. To this rectangular building, with its covered and corbelled sentry-walk, its roof so steep as to seem perpendicular, came Joan triumphant from her victory at Orleans and the immediate sequels to it: the taking of Beaugency and the battle of Patay at which Talbot was made prisoner. Her first victories, and her last. As she crossed the moat into the castle at Sully, her star passed its zenith.

This ancient part of the present Sully was the castle of the

Dauphin's favourite, Georges de la Trémoille. Flushed with success, Joan had come to carry the Dauphin off to Rheims to be crowned and consecrated. The battle of Patay had been on June 18, 1429; on the following day she had been welcomed by an almost idolatrous crowd at Orleans and had pushed straight on to Sully, where, as usual, the Dauphin was idling whilst others fought his battles. To her the issue was so simple: the way was clear for a fast journey to Rheims, where France would lose a Dauphin and gain a King.

The apathy and antagonism she had met from the Council of the Captains at Orleans should have prepared her for her reception at Sully. Charles was indolent. Kingship would have to be thrust upon him. The favourite was an avowed enemy of Joan and one who had the ear of his master at all times. The aura of success surrounding Joan won the day; a petulant and thankless Charles was borne off by the dynamic determination of the peasant girl from Lorraine. In spite of de la Trémoille, by June 24 they were on their way to Rheims.

The sweetness of the day of triumph, July 17, which saw Charles consecrated at Rheims, must have been touched with acid for Joan. Neither King nor nobles were willing that any but the barest acknowledgment should be made to her. From Rheims, Joan went forward to failure in the attempt to seize Paris, and returned next year (1430), already dispirited, to see the King again at Sully.

On the first floor of the old château is the dark and sinister room which was the King's. Next to it is an immense hall which served as an ante-chamber for the innumerable hangers-on at the rather dismal Court. Above them is another huge room, a little less sombre, with the most superb chestnut rafterwork that the Middle Ages have left us, clean in design, magnificent in workmanship if one bears in mind the tools of the time. Its cost must have been prodigious. For it were chosen trees between half a century and a century old. They were stripped on the spot and cut down in winter, when the trunks would be most free of sap. The trunks were sawn square so that only the hard core remained; at least half of the ordinarily usable wood was thus wasted. They were then weathered for several years in running water, after which they were stacked in the open to mature for several more years before being cut to length for the roof construction. The result is that after five-hundred years this splendid timberwork is as sound as the day it was put up; only some wartime bomb damage has had to be repaired (the charming village of Sully, alas, suffered heavily in 1940 and 1944).

I like to think that it was in this room, and not either of the others, that Joan met and argued with the King. There is no certainty about it, for subsequent generations have preserved the memory of the Duc de Sully, the Minister of Henri IV, rather than that of Joan. One can so easily picture her, pacing up and down with her slow, peasant stride, impatience gnawing at her soul, looking up to the rich woodwork and wishing she were out under the sky; whilst the King, so much more her debtor than his vanity would allow him to recognise, promised one day and retracted the next, according to whether the simplicity of Joan or the duplicity of de la Trémoille turned his incoherent thoughts in one direction or another. For nearly the entire month of March, 1430, she was kept there, virtually a prisoner, allowed no contact with the outside world, cut off from the people who, alone, loved her and from the open-air life in which, alone, she thrived. How much darker than to us must this great room have seemed to her, who felt entrapped by any walls other than those of a church; the glorious chestnut beams can have been to her no more than prison bars.

In April she rode out again along the banks of the Loire. In Touraine, spring lines them with infinite soft shades of greys and greens. Above the red islands the luminous sky is flecked with tiny white clouds, forerunners of the more stately ones of summer. In spite of all her disappointments, Joan must have thanked God and her Saints to be engaged again upon her life's work, the driving out of the King's enemies, in surroundings softer and more beautiful even than those of her native village. There is no record of her having been beset by the dark presentiment that, as Sully's strong white towers diminished and disappeared behind her, she had but one short month in which to enjoy her freedom before her capture by the Burgundians, and but one short year until her trial by the Church, her condemnation by Frenchmen, her burning by the English.

The old château belongs to memories of Joan; there is, however, a new one. The Petit Château was built towards the end of the sixteenth century, a Renaissance dwelling corresponding to the growing dislike of the dark, damp, feudal fortresses as places to live in, and to the desire for comfort and grace. Within a few years, the Barony and the castle were bought (1602) from the de la Trémoille family by Maximilien de Béthune.

First of the line of Ministers who made France the most powerful kingdom in the world, Maximilien was also the greatest, greater even than Richelieu. He was a more successful soldier than almost any other man of his times. Committed at an early age to the care of Henry of Navarre, his was the victory of the Protestant forces at Coutras and at Ivry.

As a Councillor he was tactful, sagacious, far-seeing. He did more than any other man to bring Henry of Navarre to his final conversion to the Catholic faith, against all his own religious principles, because he believed that France, bleeding to death from the wounds of civil war, needed his master as the only physician able to save the patient.

His success as a financier was unique. In this he far sur-
passes Richelieu, and France could have done with his like
again many times in her subsequent history. Economists
deride him because he initiated nothing, but applied existing laws. At the time he took over, less than half the taxes
of the kingdom ever reached the King's exchequer. In
thirteen years he raised the income of the State from nine
million livres to twenty million. He took over an empty
treasure chest in 1590; by 1609 there were twenty million
livres to spare. The national debt was reduced from three
hundred and fifty million livres to fifty million, in spite of
the King's heavy expenditure. Never before was France
so prosperous, and the State never has been again.

Why then is he so little known? He was a paragon, dedicated to his work; poor company and with no notorious
vices. Nobody can make him an interesting historical
figure. Virtue, alas, makes dull reading.

His first major step upwards was in 1601, when he was
made Grand Master of Artillery. To provide a proper
background to this honour, he bought Sully in the following year. Four years later, Henri IV made Sully into a
duché-pairie, and the Minister became Duc de Sully.

He survived his master by thirty-one years, mostly spent
in retirement in this château. As you step into the ground-
floor dining-room of the Petit Château, you enter what was
the writing-room of his day. He used to rise at three in the
morning; before dawn he was already at work dictating
to his four secretaries those memoirs whose very title
gives such a fascinating glimpse of the author himself:
'Memoirs of the Wise and Royal State, Domestic, Political
and Military Oeconomies of Henry the Great, the Example
of Kings, the Prince of Virtues, of Arms and of Laws, and
the effective Father of the French People; and of the Useful
Services, Proper Obediences and Loyal Administration

of Maximilien of Béthune, one of the most Familiar Con-
fidants and Useful Soldiers and Servants of the French
Mars; dedicated to France, to all Good Soldiers, and to all
the Peoples of France.'

There you have him perfectly; pompous, didactic, full
of self-importance, at once soldier and civil servant. He
never sought popularity; he still might have won it, but
for one unforgivable defect—he was always right, and that
nobody forgives. A great man, indeed, but one doubtless
insufferable to know.

In the time of his eighteenth-century descendants he must
have turned in his grave all day and most of the night. To begin
with, they played havoc with the sensible internal arrangements as he had left them, turning the study into a dining-
room and his bedroom into a Salon, and filling the house
with notorious libertines and fiercely Republican *philosophes*.

Amongst the guests was a young man who was not
quite either, one François-Marie Arouet, self-styled de
Voltaire. Wandering to and fro under the great trees of the
park, flirting with the girls and being impertinent with the
men, the young Voltaire had his first taste of life in the
great world outside Paris, from which, at 22, he had just
been exiled for insulting the Regent. He was also, though
he could not know it, within a year or so of his first imprisonment for the same offence. He was believed to have
been the author of an anonymous, and very horrid, verse
accusing the Regent of incest with the Duchesse de Berry.
To be fair to Voltaire, he strongly denied it in another verse,
on the grounds that a poet, Jesuit-trained, would know
nothing of the Moabites and Ammonites, and that his sole
knowledge of the people of the ancient world would be of
the Sodomites. The second verse is so perfect a sequel
to the first that it is difficult to believe that they were not
both by the same hand.

This, however, was still in the future. At Sully he spent

the hours not otherwise engaged in writing comedies for the guests to play, one of which at least, *Artémise*, still lives. In the immense first-floor room of the feudal château, with its vast Gothic fireplace that must have looked like the mouth of a devouring dragon when the wood logs burned in it, are to be seen the remains of the stage on which these plays were enacted.

However great his satisfaction at being entertained by dukes, crossing swords with wits and flirting with the gay young ladies, the house of Sully was to bring no ultimate satisfaction to this nastily-clever young man. He left the château under a cloud of disapproval; his cutting tongue could have made him few friends. Nevertheless, we find him, ten years later, the guest of the Duke at the Hôtel de Sully in Paris (now number 62, rue Saint Antoine). A lacquey brings him a note, entreating him to come down to the street to hear of a plot against him, something to which he is evidently well-accustomed, for without hesitation he does so. Once there he is severely caned by the servants of the Chevalier de Rohan-Chabot, who stands by laughing.

The cause was some quarrel with the Chevalier over the notorious Adrienne Lecouvreur of the Comédie Française. Voltaire took fencing lessons for six weeks, then sent in his challenge. No impertinent little writer, however clever, could challenge a Rohan with impunity. To call himself Arouet de Voltaire did not provide him with a family tree sufficient to carry the honour of allowing a Rohan to run a sword through his body. Instead of taking part in a duel, Voltaire found himself in the Bastille for a second time. After a month's reflection, he asked for, and was given, permission to leave the country. He went to London. He came back with the *Henriade*, a love of Shakespeare, and those ideas on privilege and kingship which made him, above all others, the creator of the Revolution.

The germ of these ideas must have been present already in this Château of Sully where, if the women loved him, the men would not admit him as their equal, to the great hurt of his vanity. Hurt vanity, perhaps, launches more revolutions than does idealism.

It is better to have a last look at Sully with the eyes of a Joan rather than of a Voltaire. The round towers, with the corbelled and roofed sentry-walks projecting out like the brim of a hat under a pointed crown; the straight lines and masses of the blocks joining them; and the shallow-curved lines of the steep-pitched, grey roofs, broken by a single dormer in each, are reflected in the running water of the moats, the outlines shimmering and shivering until, if you look long enough at them, it is the castle slipping by, and not the water. As she turned in the shadow and saw the castle receding, the contrast between the massive and gloomy rooms and the white and cheerful exterior must have been more striking to her, who had spent so many wasted days there, than ever it can be to us, who have done no more than spend an interesting hour musing in them. One can begin to realise that it must indeed have seemed to her a whitened sepulchre.

CHAPTER IV

The Poets

(TALCY)

UNLIKE Joan of Arc, who left Sully to follow the banks of the river towards Orleans, we cut across the great slow bend of the Loire, due east to Mer. This cross-country journey shows what a misnomer the 'Garden of France' really is, for there are substantial areas of mere and trees, and poor soil that even the French peasant cannot cultivate. To the French, the English are the most wasteful people on earth. This part of the country, the Sologne, which lies between the Val d'Orléans and the River Cher, would in England have been left as moorland. Yet as you travel through it you will see that every square foot of earth it is possible to cultivate grows something, even if it is only Jerusalem artichokes. The rabbit in England is a plague about which we do little or nothing; incredibly, for a country overrun by rabbits, we import frozen ones from Australia to eat. To the French, the wild rabbit is a valuable addition to his food (and a well-prepared *blanquette de lapin* in the Sologne is a worthy dish in a region reputed for its cooking) and the mainstay of the French furrier. I sometimes suspect them of growing the artichokes largely because hares love to make their forms amongst them, and hare makes an even better winter meal than rabbit.

The meres serve their purpose, too; we have forgotten in England that the monks (wise men in their day) bred fresh-water fish to eat. Here every pond and stream furnishes fish for the table, and a pike, well cleaned and prepared, is incomparably superior to most of the fish we get from the sea. Where the English farmer has six cows grazing in a field, you may be sure that there will be twelve French cows in a field of the same size. Where no cow can graze, goats thrive, and goat's milk cheese makes a fine dessert. By the intelligent use of marginal land England could vastly increase her production of food, and the Sologne is an excellent object-lesson as to how it might be done; even the bracken serves as cattle-litter, and goes back to fertilise the land.

Through green fields and past green woods, in sight of purple heather and the reflection of a light-blue sky in the meres, the lanes end at Mer and the Loire. Straight across the river, and six miles beyond the other side, is Talcy.

Talcy is another of the greatly underestimated châteaux, yet it is certainly fit to take place in the second rank of them, if not in the first. It was built, about 1520, by a Florentine, Bernard Salviati, cousin of Catherine de Médicis, at the time when François I was busy with the Italianate wing of the château of Blois, when everything Italian was the very height of fashion, and the transalpine architects had not yet assimilated the gentle light and delicate colourings of the Loire valley.

Yet, and in this it is almost unique, it is built away from the river in the most unpromising position of La Beauce, scorning all the natural advantages of the magnificent river setting to be found so few miles away. Built for an Italian, it is as remote from Italy as it is from Persia or Cathay. It is, almost alone of its date, uncompromisingly French. It occupies the site of a small fortress of the twelfth century, from which it inherited a certain strength; not enough to make it a fort, yet sufficient to make it a manor house easily defended.

There is a strong, square tower, surmounted by a corbelled sentry-walk and carrying three turrets with rather the
self-conscious air of a serious somebody-in-the-city wearing
a comic hat to please the children. Simple, rectangular,
unornamented almost, it stands amongst the other châteaux
(if the metaphor may be allowed to change sex) like the
county lady who, having found a style to suit her, refuses
thereafter to pander to the fashion of the day.

If the outside is uncompromising, the inner courtyard is
soft and feminine to the point of prettiness. In the middle
of it is a dome-covered well; the corner of the too-massive
keep is rendered surprisingly effeminate by a turret staircase, looking the more delicate for the direct comparison
with its heavy neighbour; the main building is lightened by
a four-arcaded gallery, severe enough for a monastery, were
it not lightened by two fanciful gables. To what extent
Bernard Salviati was ruled by his wife, history does not tell,
but the evidence of Talcy is that he arranged the exterior
to his liking, but his wife asserted her ideas when it came to
the courtyards.

The second courtyard is difficult to see, so much is it
dominated by an immense dovecote, apparently contemporary with the main building, yet still in splendid condition. It has some 1,500 pigeon-holes, if that is the right
word in a dovecote; the French *alvéoles* is distinctly more
poetic. We know that they were early risers in those days,
and well must they have needed to be at Talcy, for the
awakening of a thousand doves must have driven all but
the dead from their sleep.

The approach road from the Loire is practically featureless, and therefore timeless; fortunately, for though there
must have been changes since Catherine de Médicis approached Talcy in slow state in 1562, they are not obtrusive
enough to prevent the present-day traveller from visualising
the long procession.

First came the *fourriers*, the sutlers, whose business it was to prepare the reception of royalty; amongst them were the hundred-odd cooks and pastrycooks and *rôtissiers* and scullions, with all their kitchen paraphernalia, travelling in or alongside the provision carts. The music of the farmyard went with them, for the royal procession carried its supplies on the hoof, as it were, live sheep and oxen and fowls, to supplement such game as might be in season.

Long after this noisy, and probably smelly, crowd anxious to arrive and have time in hand for the lengthy preparation of the royal meal, came the first of the horsemen, the gentlemen-at-arms, courtiers and bodyguard at one and the same time, with multi-coloured silks and satins and velvets shining in the sun and the long feathers hanging from their hats waving in the breeze. Amongst them would be the first of the mule-drawn litters, cramped and uncomfortable, from which the more courageous and least travel-sick of the ladies would gallantly converse with the cavaliers.

After another gap would come the Royal Litter, in which the Queen reposed on cushions of white satin, but the down from all the ducks in the world under a silken cover would not have saved her from the jolting set up by the mules as they lurched in and out of the deep ruts and great holes in the road.

In the rear would come the *Gouvernante*, the official duenna or state chaperon, responsible for the good behaviour of the young ladies of the Court, many of whom were still children. Her charges included Catherine's notorious 'Flying Squad', whom contemporaries accused of being her spies, and worse. The *Gouvernante* called the roll at night, doubtless turning a blind eye and a deaf ear when one or other of her charges had to sleep out on the Queen's business. The very fact that there was a roll-call at all throws a better light on the Court; it is even possible that Catherine, whom nobody loved, was much maligned, and the dubious rôle of the 'Flying Squad' greatly exaggerated by her enemies. Its origin was not even attributable to her, but to her husband, who had no more sinister motive than an aesthetic pleasure in being surrounded by young and pretty girls to bring grace and laughter to a stuffy Court.

On this occasion, at least, Catherine appears at Talcy in the best of lights, summoning to her presence the Guise family, representing the Catholic Church Militant, and Condé, representing the Protestant Church, no whit less militant, in order to establish some sort of peace between them. There is no reason to doubt her sincere desire, at that moment at least, for internal peace; put it, if you like, at the lowest level, that she needed it in her own self-interest. But whether she walked up and down the courtyard and round and round the well with her hand resting lightly on the arm of a Guise as she besought him to take a more statesmanlike view of the New Religion, or whether she pleaded with the stern, narrow-minded, hunch-backed Condé, in one of the well-proportioned upper rooms, to restrain his followers and not to stir up further troubles, she could achieve nothing.

On both sides she had to deal with self-righteous fanatics; on both sides were men who, though far from saints, were quite prepared for martyrdom rather than to cede an inch. Both dared to call themselves Christians, both dared to receive Communion when the hearts of each were filled with hate of their fellow men of the same language, of the same race and, fundamentally, of the same religion.

Fortunately the sound of the doves at Talcy was not always drowned by voices raised in angry religious and political argument. More fittingly, it was the background to lovely verse, to the first love affair of the first of the poets of his time.

Bernard Salviati was a remarkable man. As cousin of the

Queen, he seems to have been unique in his time in not using the relationship to further his own ends; or, at least, not so much so that history records it. An Italian of the Renaissance, he let his house be built in a purely French style. As patron of the arts, he neglected his own country-men to welcome the men of letters of his adopted country. It is ironic that Talcy, scene of an historic event, and Salviati, a man of distinction in his own right, should be remembered as the home and the father respectively of a girl of whom we know little, beyond her name and the bare facts of her history, Cassandre.

She was Ronsard's first love; to her, in all probability, he wrote his first sonnet. How true of her, how all too true, were the words of another sonnet he wrote, in his vast egotism, to another well-loved lady: 'When you are very old, at dusk, by candlelight, sitting by the fireside, chatting and spinning, you will speak my verses, saying in wonder-ment, "Ronsard sang of me when I was beautiful".'

He did not marry her, probably for her good. Better to have loved and lost a poet than to be married to him; the better the poet, the worse the husband. For that matter, we do not know that she ever loved him at all. It was flattering to a young girl to inspire fine sonnets, but whether she loved the deaf poet as a man is another question. She married, but not Ronsard. Yet indirectly her link with great French poetry was to last many generations; her daughter married one Guillaume de Musset, from whom was to descend in the far future Alfred de Musset.

It is not even certain that Ronsard did more than adore an idealised Cassandre; it is a way that young poets have. All his life different women inspired him, and those who know only his verse might well believe that he was the Don Juan of his times. Both he and his friend, Joachim du Bellay, wrote as if pleasures of the senses and of the flesh were all they lived for; both lived in a fashion, for the times, quite austere morally and materially. 'They wrote like Epicures and lived like Anchorites.'

Pierre de Ronsard, born in 1524, was brought up in Courts. At the age of ten he was page to the Duke of Orleans; at twelve, he was taken into the household of James Stuart of Scotland. With him he spent over two years in Scotland, and another in England. Then he returned to the service of the Duke of Orleans.

He was twenty-four when a chance meeting at an inn on the road from Poitiers to Paris brought him into touch with Joachim du Bellay, a year his junior, the lesser poet but stronger character of the two. Joachim was born at Liré, on the Loire between Angers and Nantes. He was the son of relations of the great du Bellays. His parents died in his early boyhood and he was brought up very strictly by a much older brother.

The two poets, who had so much in common, set up what what was in effect a Poetic Academy in Paris. Others joined them (none of any great note) and the group became known as the Pleiad. Its influence on French literature and language still endures.

Curiously both these poets were deaf, and wrote each other sonnets on their deafness. Both of them, in spite of official subservience to the Church were pagans. Both wrote verse of a technical excellence that has never been excelled in French, yet neither were deep thinkers and neither fundamentally sincere.

Take Joachim's most famous sonnet; those who know French, will know it by heart; for those who do not, here is a rough translation, following the form of the original, but lacking all its graces.

> Happy the man, like Ulysses, who can attain
> A noble journey's end, or, like he who won
> The Fleece, return in wisdom, travels done,

5. AMBOISE. *The château, with the tour des Minimes: 'round a central pillar is a winding ramp . . . carefully graduated, so that a horseman may ride up it'.*

6. AMBOISE. *The Chapel of Saint Hubert: '. . . the most perfect building the final phase of French Gothic has left us is this tiny chapel . . . the Renaissance was already knocking at the door to come in'.*

And ever after with his kin remain.
Alas! When shall I see the smoke again
 Rise from my hamlet in the morning sun,
 Behold my house, precious as silver spun,
For which would I whole provinces disdain?
 Better the dwelling that my fathers made
Than Roman palace daringly array'd;
 Better my slate than marble; better, too,
  Than Tiber's flood this Gallic Loire of mine,
  My Liré hill than mountain-Palatine,
 Than rich sea air, the fragrance of Anjou.

Joachim was taken up by his great relations, and spent
many years with them in Embassy to Italian states, including
François' vain attempt to reconcile the Pope and Henry VIII
on the matter of the King's divorce. He could at any time
have come back to his house at Liré, to his Gallic Loire,
and to the fragrance of Anjou. The fact is he preferred the
luxury of Courts and the Roman palaces to the dull and
sober life of a Loire-side village. Who shall blame him?
Only those foolish enough to think that a poem does more
than to perpetuate a poet's evanescent feeling which may
have passed almost before the ink is dry on the last line of
verse.

Neither of them can be considered amongst the world's
great poets, for neither of them were revolutionaries,
and all great poets have to be that. Who did more than
Shakespeare, in his devastating portraits of bygone monarchs, to demolish the Divine Right of Kings and prepare the
way for a Cromwell (and what might he not have made of
Cromwell as protagonist of an historical play)? In any well-
organised country, poets would be suppressed at birth.
In Britain and America we are too civilised to do that;
we just let them starve to death, but then neither is a really
well organised country. But what, one wonders, happens

E

behind the Iron Curtain? Every poet is a deviationist born; one born in a revolutionary land will simply revolt against the revolution. It seems very unlikely that any great poet will emerge from Russia in our time.

However, the poet Ronsard at Talcy was the gentlest and softest-spoken of young men. I think I can see him now, eagerly clutching the fair copy of his latest sonnet, at the foot of the spiral staircase, listening to the tapping of little Cassandre's feet as she comes flying down to meet him. I see him in that feminine courtyard, reading the flowing lines with all the art Court-life has taught him, and Cassandre's oval face flushing with pleasure under her fair, wavy hair, as she hears that rather naïf and youthful tribute to her:

> Her childish beauty of her fifteen years,
> Her golden locks rippling into many a curl,
> A rose-pink brow, a fair youth's soft-hued cheeks,
> A smile that lifts my soul towards the stars;
> A virtue worthy of her beauty,
> A snowy neck, a throat of milky white,
> A heart mature within the staunchest breast,
> A very human Lady of beauty nigh divine;
> An eye so bright it makes the night seem day,
> A hand so soft it smoothes away my cares
> And in its fingers holds my very life;
>
> By a song sweetly sung,
> By a smile or a sigh,
> By such enchantments,
> Are my senses enslaved.

The cooing of the doves in the further courtyard was the music to his song. From his room that looked out over the dovecote came perhaps the germ of that fragile ode beginning 'my little lady dove', in which he compares his own love-making with the advance and retreat of the gentle birds in their mating time; of the lady's flight, not too far; of the male's pursuit; of the stolen kiss. The simile fits Ronsard better even than perhaps he knew himself.

CHAPTER V

The Windsor of France

(BLOIS)

IT is not unknown for visitors to come away from Blois
exhausted, footsore, bad-tempered and disappointed.
The extent of the castle is considerable; it is a sal-
magundi of styles, carrying you in a few yards across a
span of centuries. If you cannot, on a crowded day, get
close enough to him to catch all that the guide says, or
if your knowledge of French does not enable you to follow
his explanations with ease, then a potentially fascinating
visit can become irritating and boring. Yet Blois is intrin-
sically the most interesting and possibly the most evocative
of all the Loire châteaux. It is also the one that is most
strikingly bare, and I hope it remains so. It is too full of
ghosts to leave room for furniture, and the often chill and
uninviting interior fits much of its cold and brutal history.

The town is some fifteen miles from Talcy, downstream,
and is one of the old bridgeheads that made the Loire the
outer moat defensive of the capital. There were but seven
of them from Gien to Angers, protected by castles virtually
impregnable except by treachery. The strength of the castle
gave confidence to the inhabitants, and towns, large for the
times, grew up around them. They were wealthy towns,
deriving a substantial income from a levy on all goods
passing across the bridges. Such is the conservatism of the
French that Blois remains a substantial town to this day,

though the importance of its bridge is much diminished and
there are no tolls to add to its prosperity. There are no
visible signs of industry, and the casual visitor may well
wonder on what the twenty thousand inhabitants live,
unless it be on the proceeds of bygone centuries of levies.

The present bridge is of respectable age, but no more. It
was built to the design of Jacques-Ange Gabriel, the
restorer of the Louvre and the creator of the Petit Trianon at
Versailles. It replaced a wooden one, that was complete with
shops on either side of it, like old London Bridge. The
wooden structure was swept away by record floods. When
the new one was built in the early years of the eighteenth
century it was already the era of men whose architectural
knowledge and daring was based on the most advanced
conceptions of applied mathematics, yet it was still generally
believed even by them that a flat bridge would inevitably
collapse. The bridge at Blois, therefore, has a hump-back,
most useful for the observer. From the top of the hump
you look straight up the Rue Denis-Papin, which ends in a
most decorative, indeed monumental, stairway leading to
the heights of the upper town. To the left are still visible
the empty spaces caused by German bombing in 1940
and above them, on the height, the broken façade of the
great grey castle above a little terrace.

From here you are looking at part of the feudal enclosure,
the Tour du Foix; at all that remains of the chapel, dating
from the end of the sixteenth century; and at an end-on
view of the seventeenth-century wing in the classical
manner designed by the younger Mansart: as curious a
mixture as you are ever likely to see at a single glance.
(The younger Mansart, or Mansard, was the designer of the
dome of the Invalides, the Place Vendôme and the Place
des Victoires in Paris, and of the palace and chapel of
Versailles. Although he took the name of the illustrious
François Mansart, whose *mansardes* made attics habitable,

he was born a Hardouin and was related to him only by marriage.)

The castle faces backwards compared with most of the Loire châteaux, which were mainly built to be seen from the river. Here the finest façade looks northwards, away from the river, and it is difficult to see it completely from any viewpoint.

The story of the castle at Blois is as involved as its architecture. There had been some kind of fortress here from very early, possibly Merovingian, times. The first one, of which there is proper historical record, was built by Thibault the Trickster (to whom the keep at Châteaudun is so strangely and wrongly ascribed). The Châtillon family knocked that one down and for more than a century went on building a dark and fearsome feudal stronghold in its place. The Tour du Foix and the original part of the *Salle des Etats* (the Westminster Hall, as it were, of the times) survive from this period.

In 1391 it passed into the hands of Louis d'Orléans. His eldest son, Charles d'Orléans, the poet, inherited it. Late in life, he began to knock down the old part and to build a more civilised dwelling; the mid-fifteenth-century wing bears his name. Early in the sixteenth century, Louis XII and Anne of Brittany added a new wing. Their successor, François I, brought Italian architects to work, and left us a magnificent façade, the finest of all staircases and the most Italianate of all the Loire buildings.

Nearly a century passed before the next major alterations. Under Gaston d'Orléans, François Mansart started a complete rebuilding which was intended to do away altogether with the Renaissance building. Happily only one wing was completed. France might have gained an earlier and smaller Versailles (and I feel that one Versailles is quite enough), but would have lost a major treasure of earlier times.

You enter in the north-west through a grand doorway in

a charming frontage of combined brick and stone, both so
mellowed by time that it is difficult to visualise it in its
original brightness; it has all the irregular grace of the
times of Louis XII. The mansion of Cardinal d'Amboise,
the King's gifted Minister, faced this wing, but was
destroyed by bombing in 1940. It used to give the guide
great pleasure to point out the two balconies from which
King and Cardinal liked to carry on familiar conversations
as they took the air in the fresh of the evening, a domestic
touch delightfully at variance with the formality of later
Courts. The interior of this wing is of particular interest as it
is one of the first examples of the new style where the rooms
communicate with a gallery or corridor; until this time they
all gave into each other in succession.

The Tour du Foix, over to the extreme left as you enter,
is the only unaltered part of the castle as it was, when it
passed from the hands of the Comte de Châtillon into those
of the Orléans family. The story of this change of ownership is a wry tale; the moral, if there be one, lies as deep-
buried as in a Restoration comedy, for which it might well
have served as a model.

There is the aged, doting husband, the Comte de Châtillon, rich and powerful. There is the beautiful young wife,
relatively a nobody. There is the charming, unscrupulous
young Prince, the Duke of Orleans, brother of the King.
The wife deceives the husband; that, in the circumstances,
might almost have been expected. What is a little unusual
is that the lover, a Prince of the Blood Royal, takes money
from the wife, very considerable sums of money, which
she extorts from her husband. The years pass; there comes
a day when the rich and powerful Count is rich no longer;
his young wife has clawed his gold away from him to give
to her lover. The Count has no alternative but to sell the
château, which has always entailed the support of hundreds
of retainers. The wife may have lost her head and heart to

the Prince; he at least never lost his head. The buyer of the
château is the Prince who has always pleaded poverty to
his mistress, and carefully put by all the money with which
she has paid for his favours. Thus did Blois pass dishonour-
ably into the possession of the Orleans family.

Sixteen years later Louis d'Orléans was assassinated in
Paris, which some may feel was justice long deferred.
His widow retired to Blois. Such was the charm of this
handsome scoundrel that she died within the year, because
she felt there was nothing left for her to live for without
him, as clear a case of a broken heart as the most romantic
novelist could wish.

The château passed to Charles d'Orléans, eldest son of
Louis. England owes much to him for so handsomely
losing the battle of Agincourt. There he was made prisoner;
he spent a quarter of a century in captivity, not too unpleas-
antly engaged in writing poetry of a wistful charm.

Eventually he returned to France and to Blois, to find
himself a widower (for the second time). The story of his
father's acquisition of Blois might have warned him of the
danger of age wedding youth. He ignored it, and married
Mary of Cleves who, like Juliet, had attained the respectable age of fourteen and was thus thirty-six years his
junior.

This grim fortress, he decided, was no place for his young
wife. He knocked down part of it and built a delightful
new wing. All that you can see of this today is a simple
gallery on the courtyard, backing on to the remains of the
chapel which his son built. In these more pleasant surroundings he held a truly Renaissance Court, at which artists and
poets were his honoured guests.

To achieve his dearest desire, he had to wait one-and-
twenty years. It was not until he was seventy-one that Mary
gave birth to a son, the future King Louis XII. If there were
some who dared to doubt the child's paternity, Charles

himself was not amongst them; however much the tongue of scandal might wag in private, nothing was said in public to cast aspersions on the child's legitimacy.

So Louis XII succeeded his cousin Charles VIII on the throne, and inherited Blois from his father. His equestrian statue stands over the portal through which you enter, for this first wing you visit was his. It is a fairly faithful modern reproduction of the original statue destroyed during the Revolution. Perhaps the wing belongs more to his down-to-earth wife, Anne of Brittany, whose emblem, an ermine, is as much to be seen on the decoration as the porcupine of her husband.

The courtyard frontage is as delightful as the stone-and-brick exterior façade. The ground floor is an open gallery, the arches of which are supported alternatively by pillars decorated with the fleur-de-lys and by columns most delicately arabesqued, a foretaste of the more flamboyant Renaissance decoration to come in the next generation. For the first time France knew internal peace under a Valois King. That Louis was much influenced both by Cardinal d'Amboise and by his dull but strong-minded wife, cannot be doubted, but his own natural gifts of tolerance and spiritual generosity bring him into vivid contrast with his predecessors. The livelier spirits complained that the Court was a bourgeois one and greatly disliked the severe Queen Anne. This wing, in its simplicity (but for the royal emblems it might well have been the manor house of a not-too-important noble) reflects the quiet times. There was war, indeed, in Italy; but that war was the last flowering of chivalry. On the one side was Bayard, 'the knight without fear and without reproach'; on the other, Gonzalvo de Córdoba, 'the cream and flower of chivalry'; on both sides there were the last great deeds of noble knights.

Of the great terraced gardens designed by Pacello, whom Charles VIII brought over from Italy, there remains today only a tiny terrace, the one spot from which the fine north façade of the château can be seen. The rest have vanished to make way for the modern streets in the town. Their loss is disastrous, for they were the reason for the castle facing as it does; Blois without them is as if the approach to Versailles had been built over, up to within a street's width of its frontage.

The definite gardens did not, properly speaking, come into being until Louis XII brought Mercogliano to lay them out, in 1499. They were completed in 1510, as far as a garden can ever be said to have been completed. They were either the first, or at least very nearly the first, of their kind in France. The nearest approach to them to be seen today is at Villandry, which I shall describe in a later chapter; but some account of the gardens at Blois will give an idea of the pattern which those of every other château followed in greater or lesser degree, and greater rather than lesser.

At Blois the ground rose gently towards the east. Mercogliano took advantage of this natural feature to place the gardens on three levels. This architectural conception, this three-dimensional treatment, is the basis of all Renaissance gardens. In part this was due to the age, an age in which art was essentially architectural. In part it was a development of the oriental terrace-system of irrigation. Mostly it could be attributed to the third factor, the lack of colour in the early Renaissance garden. The attraction had to reside mainly in pattern; the gardener was forced to be an artist in line and not in colour, because the development of the innumerable shades of leaf and flower with which we are familiar was still to come, mostly much later.

In fact, all the designer of this period had as basic material for his garden were simple creepers and climbing plants and roses little removed from the wild state, such plants as we have now relegated to the kitchen garden, and the aromatic bushes and herbs, thyme and lavender and mar-joram.

The Blois gardens were on three levels; at the lowest, nearest the château, was the original one, refashioned by Mercogliano. It was bounded on the side away from the château by an essential of the times, the Orangery. This was a decorative building, the upper storey being the Orangery proper, and the lower being used as gardeners' dwellings. Four square beds, subdivided into geometrical patterns, were on the nearer side, with a fountain where the paths crossed in the middle. Beyond the Orangery were the *Jeux de Paume*, the fives-courts of the time.

This was the smallest garden of the three. The middle one, immediately above it, was Mercogliano's own creation, far more complex. It was reached from the château by a gallery decorated with trophies of the chase. In its turn the gallery led to a pavilion, and the pavilion to the garden proper, surrounded by wooden galleries, creeper-covered. Ten varied patterns composed it, outlined with shaped yews (like the quite common, colourful garden plants of today, the characteristic box bushes of the French-style gardens did not come into use for another hundred years), and filled in with carefully ordered herbs and aromatic bushes.

The third, the High Garden, much greater in area than the other two, was far enough away from the château to call for less minute detail; part of it was the kitchen garden, no less formal and hardly less decorative than the pleasure garden, with geometrical arrangements of lettuce and endive and asparagus and white mulberry (the artichoke, so prom-inent a feature a few generations later, is believed to have been introduced by, of all unlikely people, Rabelais in 1537).

In the very centre of the High Garden was a noria, a water-wheel turned by oxen, which drew the water needed for the fountains of the two lower gardens and for irrigation. Later an avenue of elms was added, leading to the distant forest, the first example of the use of perspective in this connection.

Such was the first pattern of a French garden: formal, geometrical, architectural. Not until architecture had reached the virtual limit of its development within the possibilities of the materials available before the industrial age, did the informal, the non-architectural garden and the English park of soft contours and distant vistas, with a natural air resulting from well-concealed art, come into fashion.

After the domestic virtues of Louis and Anne, the flamboyance of François I is the more striking. His wing, which adjoins the *Salle des Etats*, is in date only twelve years later than that of his father. In those twelve years a revolution in taste and ideas had taken place; the Renaissance had arrived.

Louis XII, to the great advantage of his kingdom, had been a careful spender, however generous he might have been of spirit; his successor was lavish. The hangings for one room alone cost François over 25,000 livres, an unheard of sum, and everything else about his château of Blois was on the same scale of magnificence.

The Renaissance wing is incomplete; part of it was knocked down by Mansart to make way for his later classical building. The result is that the great staircase is no longer central, as it was designed to be. On the whole, this has less importance than might have been the case, owing to the asymmetry of the building. Windows here are put in to give light to particular rooms, not to make a symmetrical frontage; and they are wide or narrow according to practical needs; and pilasters are used not only to frame window embrasures, but to relieve plain exterior surfaces whenever the architect thought it necessary. The decoration of the stone-work is rich and varied, the King's salamander prevailing.

The constant recurrence of emblems is a reminder that this was still an age into which the heraldry of the Middle Ages persisted; as the years go by, however, the purely pictorial design is more and more often combined with initials. Louise de Savoie, the mother of François, used as her symbol a swan pierced by an arrow, which, one would have thought, was singularly unfitting for her character. Her daughter-in law, the poor Claude de France, used a similar emblem flanked by a crown-surmounted 'F' on one side and 'C' on the other. The pure white swan, pierced through by an arrow, was in her case much more suitable to the innocent wife of a neglectful, woman-chasing husband. Claude also inherited the ermine-emblem of Anne of Brittany, but seldom used it. The fire-breathing salamander of François was almost the last of these pictorial devices to be used. Thereafter, the alphabetical device, such as the two letters 'D' of Diana of Poitiers, arranged back to back, became universal.

The interior decoration of the apartments is no less rich than the exterior. It has been, on the whole, ably restored, but suffers from an unexpected defect. It remains too new. There can be no doubt that, as first completed in the time of François, it was as colourful as it is now; it is impossible to believe that the designers, knowing their own times, expected it to remain that way. They knew that the bright newness of the colours would not last more than a few weeks. The wood smoke from the great chimney-pieces, the greasy smoke from innumerable candles, the resinous smoke of the torches, would soon cover over the apparent crudeness of their colouring. At the time of the restoration this was not taken into account. What you see now is the decoration in its original state, before the rooms had been lived in, and it clashes with the architecture for that very reason.

What is fascinating about this wing is that it is almost the earliest example of living-rooms that are both vast and light. The Gothic hall was vast enough, but in a dark and cavernous way. Here there are windows enough to be both sources of sufficient daylight and an integral part of the architectural conception. Not since the days of the scribes' room (described usually as the knights' room) in the Mont-Saint-Michel, had such use been made of window-daylight.

The stupendous staircase, which fathered so many other noble ones, is probably Blois' best-known feature, a most interesting development of the mediæval spiral. Instead of the staircase being contained within a cylindrical tower, as was the case with the spiral design, it has an octagonal container, three sides of which are let into the frontage while five sides project into the courtyard. The cage is an open-work one, cut away so as to leave pillars at each exterior angle, the stairs and balustrade making, in effect, a sloping bridge from pillar to pillar.

The staircase served a double purpose; it gave plenty of room for the hundreds of people who were perpetually going up and down, from one floor to another, and, when there was any ceremony going on in the courtyard, it served also as a grandstand (hence the five sides looking outwards). At all times it gave ample space for an imposing array of guards.

Anne of Brittany died at Blois in 1514, and in the same year François married her daughter Claude, his distant cousin. It was a marriage of convenience; it might well have been a love match on Claude's side, for the young François was a gay and handsome fellow; but she, alas for her, was too like her sober-minded mother to please this youthful Prince who had at his feet the most beautiful women in France.

No cloth of gold, no fine silks, decorated Saint-Germain for the wedding. There was even no wedding feast; for as soon as the ceremony of making them man and wife was over, François changed his dress and rode off for his usual sport of hunting in the forest.

Thus it came about that a few days later there arrived a pitiful procession at Blois. A plain and sad-faced bride, 'her face spoiled with weeping,' returned to her old home with the retinue of a petty nobleman's wife, not that of the first lady of the land. Lumbering, creaking, groaning up the steep hill to the castle came the solitary wagon carrying her new possessions. Amongst the wedding gifts, beneath its hood, was the paltry present from her husband, 'a four-post bed, and a counterpane', an expression of contempt.

François, only twenty-one when he came to the throne in 1515, carried on the war in Italy with, at first, enormous success. His victory at Marignano was the end of the reputation of the Swiss as soldiers. François was knighted on the scene of the battle by the legendary Bayard. After his capture of Milan, which started off a two-century war with the Hapsburgs, he played with the idea of an alliance with England. Henry VIII received him at Canterbury; François returned the compliment at the Field of the Cloth of Gold. Then, in 1525, the battle of Pavia showed how certainly the age of chivalry in war had departed; it was lost by him to the Spanish harquebusiers; from thenceforth, infantry fire-power and not individual knightly prowess, would determine the fate of battles. All the veterans of the Italian wars were amongst the 10,000 French dead. François was taken prisoner and carried off to Spain. 'Of all things', he wrote to his mother, 'there remains to me only honour, and my life which has been spared.'

After giving many promises, which he never had any intention of keeping, on the grounds that they were extorted by force, he returned to France, and gay Court life was revived at Blois.

Unlike his immediate predecessor, who was surrounded by men of the sword and solid bourgeois, François brought to the Court more poets, musicians and artists than even his great-uncle before him. The Maids of Honour who, under Anne of Brittany, were as severely disciplined as if they had been at boarding school, became the great attraction of the new Court. From this time onwards, feminine influence was to be all-powerful, until the end of the French monarchy. To give some idea of the King's state at that time, it is estimated that while the Court was in residence at Blois, some 15,000 people were directly and indirectly supported by it.

In 1547 François died at Rambouillet, and was succeeded by the son he despised, Henri II. "I do not like," he said on one occasion, "dreamy, sullen and sleepy children", and Henri was all three.

Of the two women who dominated France between them for so long, Diana of Poitiers and Catherine de Médicis, only the latter has any real part in this château of Blois. She was intensely disliked in her time, for many reasons. She was Italian. She was the daughter of a noble house which owed its nobility to its skill in commerce rather than in arms. She had the same passion for facing two ways at once that characterised Queen Elizabeth I. In both cases not the most intimate counsellors could flatter themselves that they really knew the Queen's mind. The English Queen was fortunate in that there was no actual war of religion in England and that its growing commercial prosperity brought a glow to her reign which time has not diminished. To the strictly impartial observer there is a curious similarity between the two Queens, though the one goes down in history as a 'good' and the other as a 'bad' Queen. Both could, and did, sacrifice their friends and supporters for political advantage. Both had tortuous minds and a love of intrigue. Both loved the exercise of power. Both went back on their words if they saw the least advantage in doing so (if you have the slightest doubt about this

7. CHANTELOUP. *'There it is, the only pagoda in the world with a colonnade, four wrought-iron balconies, and Louis XVI style decorations throughout.'*

8. CHENONCEAU. *'Behind drawbridge and keep, a bridge leads to the château proper, built upon the twin bank-abutments of an antique mill linked by a narrow arch.'*

being true of Elizabeth of England, re-read the story of her dealings with the Protestants of the Netherlands).

On the first floor of the Renaissance wing of Blois is the Cabinet of Queen Catherine. The carved wood panels are supposed to number 237, amongst which four are in reality doors to secret cupboards. The most fantastic stories have been current about these; in them Catherine was supposed to keep her store of poisons. There is not the slightest reason to believe that she ever poisoned anybody, directly or indirectly, no evidence whatsoever that she dabbled in chemistry in our sense of the word (though she may have done so in the more philosophical aspects of alchemy), and she certainly had no use for four cupboards full of poison. The alternative explanation is that these hiding places were for her jewels.

There is a much more probable explanation that does not seem to have found its way into the official histories. Catherine de Médicis brought to the Court of her father-in-law the fashion for unguents and face paints. She was never a beautiful woman, but all witnesses agree that she kept a youthful face almost to the end. Her secret cupboards most probably held those creams and lotions and powders and colours, basically identical with those still sold (many of them at prices worthy of an Elixir of Life) and which are still surrounded with a lot of the quack-scientific mystery of the alchemist turned beauty specialist. These were her profound secrets she was not going to divulge to anybody, and most particularly to her rival, Diana of Poitiers, whose spies she believed to be everywhere.

The fashion she had introduced found one unexpected prophet. From far Salon, in Provence, came a book, *Traité des Fardemens*, a Treatise on Cosmetics, by Michel de Nostradame, better known to history as Nostradamus.

All the Medici believed in astrology, and Catherine no less than the rest of her family. She had one rather notorious

F

astrologer of her own, Ruggieri; he seems to have been a complete fake. Were it not for Nostradamus, one would say that they all were, but he confounds us. This doctor of medicine, brought up to Jewish mysticism (though nominally a staunch Catholic), published in his own lifetime a series of visions of things to come that are, in so many cases, of such extraordinary accuracy as to put chance out of consideration in attempting to account for them.

Here, for example, is what he had to say of Catherine herself: 'The Lady shall be left alone in the Kingdom of her only spouse, dead before her on the Field of Honour; seven years of exploring sorrow, then long life for the happiness of the kingdom.' It is entirely accurate; after the death of her husband, in the tournament, Catherine did not remarry; she kept official mourning for seven years; she lived long thereafter. There may be two opinions as to whether it was for the good of the kingdom, but a consultant of the Queen could hardly say otherwise; and bad as was the state of France whilst she still held the reins in the lifetime of her sons, it might easily have been far worse without her. There is room here for only one more quotation, regarding her eldest son, François II: 'First son of Widow; unhappy marriage, with no children; two Islands in discord; before eighteen, incompetent age; the other near to him will make a (marriage) vow at an even lower one.' François died six weeks before attaining his majority at eighteen. His girl-wife, Mary, Queen of Scots, bore him no children; she returned to the British Isles to a lifetime of discord; François' younger brother, Charles IX, was affianced to Elizabeth of Austria at the age of eleven, although he did not in fact marry her until he was twenty.

It was not very safe in those days for an astrologer, and a Jew, to be too precise in foretelling disaster to royalty; hence the kind of shorthand in which he makes his prophecies. Even then, that of the death of Henri II is unmistakable, as is that of his own death, and both are foretold with such accuracy of detail as make it probable that, dimly, he 'saw' the future. The nearer the events are to his own times, the clearer and more accurate the description. I am personally completely convinced that in his trances (induced by a water bowl) he did see past and future in the manner J. W. Dunne described as taking place in dreams in *An Experiment with Time*, though this is not the place to develop my reasons.

In any case, these predictions were all made during the lifetime of Henri II; they first appeared in 1555, and this is substantiated beyond all possibility of argument.

Such was his fame, that Catherine persuaded Henri to invite the sage to come to Court. He arrived in Paris in the summer of 1556, and went immediately to see the King and Queen at Saint-Germain-en-Laye. Evidently he impressed them, for when he returned to Paris he was treated with great honour and lodged at the Hôtel de Sens. In due course he received a Royal Command to proceed to Blois to meet them again. Catherine wished to consult him; Catherine wanted him to cast the horoscopes of the entire family. That much is history.

Without any reason I can advance for it, I associate this meeting in my mind with Catherine's Cabinet; one can only say that it might well have been there that the grave, bearded Jew, who had already foreseen the death of the father and of the eldest son, worked out with meticulous care the conjunctions of the planets. He, who knew too much from his pre-vision, can hardly have believed in the work he was doing then. He dared not tell his royal mistress the truth. Her husband would be dead within three years, her eldest son within four. The second son would reign, and future generations would look upon him with abhorrence for the massacre of Saint Bartholomew. The little Elizabeth would become the child-wife of Philip of Spain, and lose her soul in the gloom of the Spanish Court. The third son would reign also, assassinate within these castle walls, and in his turn be assassinated. That day Nostradamus must have wished that he had never been cursed with the gift of foresight. The exquisite wood carvings, the ten score panels all different, all little masterpieces, were no proper background for such disclosures.

Whatever he did tell her was agreeable to her ears, for eight years later the widow, accompanied by the fourteen-year-old Charles IX and the ten-year-old Henry of Navarre, by thirty-five members of the 'Flying Squad' and 800 others, arrived at Salon to see him. So much to see him and none else, that during the official reception by the notables of the district the young King impetuously called out, 'I came to see Nostradamus', and the ceremony had quickly to be curtailed.

Above the Cabinet, on the second floor, reached by the staircase still known as the *Escalier des Quarante-Cinq*, is the suite of Henri III, scene of the celebrated assassination of Henri, Duc de Guise, which it is possible to retrace almost exactly. Over the generations, the power of the Guise family had grown to rival, and in their own minds to surpass, that of the King himself. They represented the ultra-Catholic group, who had no desire for peace with the Reformed Church.

They were remarkable men, these Guise Cardinals and Dukes and, but for their pride and ambition, great men. The great era of the dynasty began with Claude de Lorraine, Duc de Guise (1496-1550) who married Antoinette de Bourbon and served with François I against the Emperor Charles V. His eldest son, François de Lorraine, Duc de Guise, was an even more eminent soldier, took a leading part in the wars of religion, and was assassinated by a militant Protestant. Two of his brothers became, like their father's brother, Cardinals. François, nicknamed *Le Balafré*, 'Scarface', was the defender of Metz, drove the English from Calais, and was the author of the horrible massacre of the Protestants at Wassy. After his murder in 1563, he was succeeded by his son, Henri de Guise, who in turn also bore the name of 'Scarface'. He was the author of the massacre of Saint Bartholomew. His youngest brother, Louis, also became a Cardinal.

First the Guise family forced the King to hold the States General in the old *Salle des Etats* in 1576, to urge the complete suppression of the new faith. Through temporising, through playing one party off against another, Henri III held off the Guises for twelve long years. Then for a second time, they forced him to hold States General, and again at Blois. This time the Duke had taken his precautions; the 500 deputies had, in their great majority, promised him their support; the King was to be put aside. Was not the Guise claim to the throne as good as that of Henri III? Was not the Duke acclaimed by many as the greatest general, the greatest man of his times, incomparably better fitted for the throne than the vicious Henri? Guise made one mistake; he forgot how a trapped rat will fight for life and become a most dangerous enemy.

On December 23, Guise was waiting in the Council Chamber for an interview with the King. He had been up most of the night, according to report, with a lady of the 'Flying Squad', taken an hour or two of sleep, and risen again at six. It was now eight in the morning, and the waiting Duke was cold and hungry. He leaned against the huge mantelpiece, taking mouthfuls from his comfit box. On the further side of the huge fireplace was the Old Cabinet, but there was no door between the two rooms, and access to the latter could only be through the King's bedroom. (The Old Cabinet was destroyed to make room for the Mansart wing.) The King's secretary came to inform Guise that the King awaited him in the Old Cabinet. Guise left the Council Chamber by the door leading to the bedroom. Eight out of the forty-five 'gentlemen' (who were little more than paid assassins in the service of the King) were waiting there. Guise saluted them. He turned to his left, past the bed, towards the passage through the thickness of the wall into the Old Cabinet. The King, unseen, waited in the New Cabinet, to the Duke's right. The Duke opened the door into the passage, and drew back as he saw men waiting there with swords drawn. The original eight pressed in upon him, cutting off his retreat, wrapping his own cloak round his sword, clinging to arms and legs. With the strength of desperation he overthrew four of the assassins, and smashed the jaw of a fifth with his comfit box. The others leaped upon him. Covered with wounds, he staggered to the wall of the New Cabinet, then fell forever at the foot of the bed.

Then, and then only, did the King step out from his hiding place. He leant down and slapped the face of the corpse, and turned away with a shudder, remarking, 'God! How big he is. He seems even bigger dead than living.'

Catherine de Médicis was waiting in her Cabinet below, the pretty Cabinet with the lovely wood carving. The King hurried in, to tell his mother gaily, 'I have no companion now; the King of Paris is dead.'

First Saint Bartholomew, to get rid of the too-powerful Protestants; then, on almost the eve of Christmas, assassination of the too-powerful Guise. There still remained a Guise, though. The Cardinal of Lorraine, the Duke's brother, was hurried away to a cell. The next day, Christmas Eve, he too was killed. The bodies were burnt and their ashes flung over the Loire on that strange Christmastide.

The potential rivals to the throne now dead, Monarchy seemed safe. Safe it was, for eight months. Henri III was then assassinated in his turn; and with his successor,

Henry of Navarre, a new and healthier wind blew through France.

The bright and cheerful apartments of François I were no fit setting for these dark deeds, yet the mildest-mannered of us find a certain satisfaction in treading again today in the last dying footsteps of the proud Guise.

There remains only to see the gigantic proportions of the classic wing of Mansart, part of a scheme which was to include not only all the present château, but far beyond, and to be linked by a series of terraces with the distant forest. It is very sober, very elegant, very reminiscent of Versailles, and a blot on the landscape in its present situation.

Gaston d'Orléans had it built because, in his mind, it would one day be a royal palace. He was the brother of Louis XIII, and forever conspiring against him. To keep him busy, Louis made him Count of Blois, and promised him the money to rebuild the château and, incidentally, to keep him out of Paris. Gaston, delighted at getting a great deal for nothing, called in Mansart. The work went on apace for three years; to knock down the old and build the new in thirty-six months would be no mean achievement, even in these days when every possible mechanical aid can be employed in large-scale building.

Then, unexpectedly, the situation changed. After all hope had long been given up, an heir to the throne was born. With a future Louis XIV already in existence, the chance of Blois ever becoming a royal palace was virtually eliminated. Richelieu, who had recognised the value of this scheme to keep Gaston out of the way, and who may very well have proposed it to his royal master, jumped at the opportunity of saving his precious gold, and financial supplies were immediately cut off.

Gaston, in his old age, retired to Blois, but not to his new building. With more sense than he had shown during the rest of his life, he chose the Renaissance wing. He died well, much better than he had lived. With him died also the royal connection with Blois.

I have mentioned the bareness of Blois. There are two exceptions. In the *Salle des Etats* hang six splendid tapestries of the sixteenth century, relating the history of the Emperor Constantine, from cartoons by Rubens. They are interesting in themselves, but too mannered in the taste of their day to fit this feudal hall. On the first floor of the Louix XII wing is a museum. As a museum it is a perfectly good one, even for France where provincial museums and art galleries set a very high standard, but in this setting eighteenth-century paintings are quite out of place. Anything quite as incongruous as Boucher and Greuze against a late fifteenth-century background would be hard to imagine. Unfortunately there are only a handful of sixteenth-century paintings; more of their kind would have embellished this wing and given it life and colour.

Of all the memories of Blois, are there any more charming than those of the arrival of the young Fleurange, when Louis XII was King? One day, his amused courtiers advised him that a sturdy youngster, of only some eight or nine years of age, had arrived from far Lorraine, and demanded audience. The kindly King received him with due solemnity. The well-mannered boy made a courtly obeisance; the King asked him, gently, why he had come. 'To serve the greatest Prince in Christendom,' replied the precocious infant, who added that his sword and his lance were ever at the King's orders, and that he had no greater desire than to serve against the King's enemies in the King's armies. Whatever amusement this infantile champion of the Crown of France may have caused him, the King hid it, and replied, after consideration. 'My son, you are very welcome. You are yet a little young to serve me, so I will send you to Monsieur Angoulême (then the heir-apparent, the future François I) at Amboise, since he is your own age.'

So the little lad, his disappointment mitigated by the thought of having a princely companion with whom to exercise his arms, was kept for a day or two at Blois, to restore him after his long ride across France, and sent 'with many gentlemen to attend him' to play at Amboise.

CHAPTER VI

La Chasse et la Chasseresse

(CHEVERNY AND CHAUMONT)

L*A Chasse* is an all-inclusive term in France, combining both hunting and shooting in every form; its importance in French life is difficult for the foreigner to understand. There is no September season at the seaside resorts in France, because Monsieur is due to go off to *la chasse*. The garage hand, the hairdresser's assistant, the banker, the baker, the managing director, the civil servant, all spend autumn Sunday afternoons *à la chasse*. In Great Britain there is nothing comparable to its universality, and even the United States cannot show anything approaching the same proportion of men engaged in the delights of the chase. France is still a very rural country, and *la chasse* attracts a surprising number of townsmen of every social class.

In the lower levels, *la chasse* is amazing to the English-speaking world. Rabbits and hares are welcome prey, but little that moves and nothing that flies is entirely disdained, with the result that French visitors to Britain are astonished at the number and the tameness of wild birds. *La chasse* is accompanied by a considerable number of personal accidents of a minor nature, due in part undoubtedly to the alfresco lunch always associated with it; the picnic is gargantuan, and calls for large quantities of wine to wash it down. Shooting tends to be somewhat erratic thereafter.

It has also struck me that personal accidents are more numerous when the day has been a poor one for legitimate targets; I am far from suggesting that there is any deliberately accidental shooting into the human anatomy, but at least there is a tendency to let fly at anything moving without first stopping to ensure that it is not a member of the party engaged in extremely private business behind a hedge. '*Je m'excuse, j'ai cru voir un cul-blanc*', is an ancient and ever-fruitful jest, 'I'm sorry, I thought I saw a wheat-ear', for, separately, the last two words can also mean 'white bottom'. Such an incident gives rise to delightful argument and discussion for weeks afterwards, with roars of applause when the victim's chair at his favourite café is piled high with cushions whenever he enters.

This form of *la chasse* is, to us, something quaintly different and entertaining, bringing Daudet's tales of Tartarin almost within the bounds of possibility. At the other extreme, *la chasse* is formal and decorative to an extent that even traditionalist England does not know. It is ruled by a protocol more strict than any the diplomats have ever devised. It has been handed down, unaltered, from the great days of the French monarchy.

From time immemorial the forests and moorlands of Touraine have been the hunting preserves of King and nobleman. The ancient, colourful ritual of the *Grands Equipages de Chasse*, the huntsmen with their horns, the pure-bred packs, the perfectly dressed riders, the splendid horses, are a sight to thrill even those who most profoundly disagree with blood sports. This, of course, is stag hunting, not the half-humorous shooting of small birds. Summer visitors to the Loire valley can never see this ceremonial sport; so the next best thing is to visit the Hunting Museum at Cheverny.

About eight miles south-west of Blois, Cheverny is a gem. Compared to the royal châteaux, Blois, Amboise or

Chambord, it is a miniature; no more than the country house of a wealthy nobleman compared to a king's palace. Yet none of the great ones can rival Cheverny's claim to have belonged to the same family in unbroken line since the sixteenth century, though it is true that in more recent years it has passed to the elder branch of the Hurault family.

The present buildings, unlike most others in this part of the world, were virtually erected at one time (they were completed in 1634), and not refashioned from older ones. There was a predecessor, but on the site of the present outbuildings. Architecturally, it marks the transition from the Renaissance to the classical age.

It is a model of regularity: outer west block, three windows wide, three windows high; inner west block, three windows wide, two windows high; centre block, one window wide, three windows high; inner east block, two windows high, three windows wide; outer east block, three windows wide, three windows high. The dormers follow a similarly regular pattern. The approach through the park is nearly four miles long and, of course, in a dead straight line. There is the most formal of gardens in front, and the steps to the front entrance form three sides of a truncated pyramid. It is, as Mr. Cobb wrote in another connection, 'pluperfect, like a Bostonian who has been to Harvard, or an egg twice boiled.' Its concession to the Renaissance is a series of statues between the windows: they are of Roman Emperors who wear, as well they might, an air of mild amazement at finding themselves in so incongruous a place.

The luxuriance of the interior is an object lesson to Hollywood in sheer magnificence. It is the very kind of thing that decorators try to achieve in film sets when they only succeed in producing masterpieces of bad taste. Cherverny is a masterpiece of good taste, too rich for my liking, but impeccable of its kind. The superbly painted ceilings, the decorated chimney-pieces, the Gobelins tapes-

tries, all dealing with classical subjects, rival Versailles
in all but sheer size and quantity. The King's bedroom,
made evidently to convey to His Majesty that his subjects,
too, had their own visions of magnificence, gives an impression of the wealth of the seventeenth century perhaps all
the more profound for being in manor house and not in
palace. The Comte de Vibraye, the present owner, is indeed
to be congratulated on maintaining a château, unique in its
decoration and furnishings, and in permitting the public
to visit the greater part of it.

The Hunt Museum is in the outbuildings. It is decorated
with two thousand stag heads, a quite extraordinary collection of trophies of the chase. In their vast quantity they are
curiously decorative, patterning walls and pillars with the
same slightly irregular designs as make the bare twigs and
branches of a great tree in winter. They frame great photo-
graphic enlargements of scenes of the chase. Here *la chasse*
is seen in all its formal glory until you can expect the very
hounds themselves to pursue their quarry in regular and
unbroken formation of couples. The sight of them brings
back the sad-sweet sound of the French hunting horn,
heard from afar beneath the trees of the forest on a misty
winter morning.

When the hunt meets at Cheverny, the members are
greeted by a fanfare of *cors de chasse*, those coiled horns of
melancholy note ('how sad is the sound of the horn, at
dusk, from the depths of the woods . . .' was de Vigny's
thought), but there is nothing sad about the hunt itself.
As for the huntsmen, they are a gay sight, five in blue coats,
five in pink, on a dull autumn day. The real excitement of
the hunt, I understand, is when a wild boar is raised (there
are quite a few boar heads amidst the forest of antlers in
the museum), a dangerous and often unpredictable creature
who seldom meets his death without injury to hounds and
sometimes to huntsmen as well.

Yet this highly formal hunting has one thing in common with the more plebeian variety; the picnic lunch plays a most important part in it. I remember hearing, in the decade following World War I, when the Duchesse d'Uzès was the *Diane Chasseresse* of France, eternally young, once mounted upon a horse, in spite of the toll of passing years, that even she would let the huntsmen go on alone to the kill if the boar had been so inconsiderate as not to let itself be overtaken by the hounds before the sacred hour of lunch had come. Partly, doubtless, it was politeness towards those guests who might be feeling hungry, for she graced the world with her perfect courtesy, but partly also it would have been out of deference to the tradition, found all through the social scale, that the alfresco meal is as important as the hunt itself.

A complete contrast to Cheverny is Fougères, eight miles south-east and a century and a half earlier in date. Fougères is the last, almost, of the stern Gothic fortresses, lightened a little by the windows pierced in its thick walls a hundred years after it was built, but still cold and forbidding. Four-square, with one huge round tower and two smaller ones, and an immense rectangular keep, it is the very embodiment of military strength, worth a momentary stop to philoso-phise over the uselessness and ugliness of things military outmoded; but it has no grace inside to retain the visitor, only an atmosphere of desuetude and loneliness and imper-sonality. It is but ten miles more to Chaumont; so happily and peacefully we survey the valley of the Loire which we thus reach once again.

Chaumont is made up of the river, one street, and the castle. The village, with splendid irregularity, straggles along the one street parallel to the river; its houses and shops, of all ages, look as though they badly need a coat of paint; until a moment's reflection gives rise to a mental picture of the perfectly horrid appearance they would have if they were all shining with bright new colour. In their present state they are part of the landscape, they blend with it, and it would not do to have them otherwise. A winding path leads up the side of the wooded hill on which stands the château.

The early history of Chaumont is largely one of quarrels between its owners, the Amboise family, and the Crown, and ends with Louis XI pulling it down as a punishment in 1465. However, the Amboise family got it back again, and started rebuilding it almost immediately, and completed it in 1510. It stands in a park, and is all round towers, steep roofs, and tall chimneys, a compromise between fortress and dwelling-house. It was once four-square, like Fougères, but in the eighteenth century the north wing was pulled down so that now the great courtyard looks out over pleasant terraces. Unfortunately, the north-west corner was rebuilt a hundred years ago, and is not worthy of the rest.

Henri II died in 1559; his by no means disconsolate widow, Catherine de Médicis, found herself for the first time in a position of real power. Although her children had largely been brought up by Henri's mistress, Diana of Poitiers, their obedience to their mother was absolute. Whoever was to be nominally King of France, Catherine was to be the real sovereign.

This born intriguer, this Italian whom her contemporaries accused of being a poisoner and for whom no epithet was considered too outrageous, was now in a position to take revenge upon her hated rival. Diana, for all her friends at Court, must have felt her neck in danger. She had, in her time, been all-powerful; the late King was known to have done nothing without her advice. It is not possible to be all-powerful without making enemies; her friends were all too likely to prove fair-weather ones. Quickly she retired from Court, lest the hand of the Queen she had displaced and flouted strike in immediate anger.

If Catherine was the evil woman she has been painted, her revenge was a very mild one. She ordered her rival to return the jewels the King had given her; royal jewels were, in a sense, state property in those days, and her action could not be judged unreasonable on any grounds. For the moment, that was all.

Next year Catherine bought Chaumont.

Only the east wing apartments may be visited, and there you may see 'Queen Catherine's bedroom' and 'Ruggieri's room'. The former, with a fine canopied bed, furniture and tapestries of the time of Louis XIII, may well look much as it did in her day, but there is at least much doubt if it really was the room in which she slept. As for the Ruggieri room (interesting because of the portrait of the astrologer and two pictures of the Queen that hang there), this is pure imagination. Nobody can disprove that it was used by him, but, equally, nobody can prove that it ever was. It would have been a singularly cold and uncomfortable one, in a corner tower, with walls over eight feet thick; but perhaps the theory is that as he might have been experimenting with alchemy and the preparation of love philtres and the philosopher's stone, the walls would have stood up to any ensuing explosion. Such explosions were not unknown in alchemists' laboratories.

The Catherine de Médicis 'traditions' attached to Chaumont seem almost all to be the inventions of romancers. Catherine did not buy Chaumont to live in it herself. She bought it to do a deal with her ex-rival.

Diana had immured herself in Chenonceau, keeping very quiet indeed. The fact that the Queen's revenge was long coming can hardly have added to her tranquillity of spirit. Chenonceau, though not as lovely under Diana as it was to become later, was more desirable as a residence than Chaumont.

So the second, and the last, part of Catherine's revenge

for all the years during which the older woman had taken the Queen's rightful place as the King's chief counsellor, as the supervisor of his legitimate children's upbringing, as the sharer of his intimate life, as the first lady in the land, was to make her exchange a more beautiful château for a larger and less lovely one.

This was really Christian forbearance whatever the reason may have been; one of the most remarkable examples of it, from woman to woman, that history records. Yet the historians would have us believe that Catherine was one of the worst characters in a cruel and bloody period. There are times when one is tempted to agree with Henry Ford that 'history is bunk'.

So Chaumont, usually associated with Catherine, is essentially the château of Diana; Chenonceau, which one first thinks of as essentially Diana's, owes far more to Catherine than to her predecessor.

You enter Chaumont in the south-east corner, between two of its grand round towers, over a drawbridge. Above the portal are the arms of France and the initials of Louis XII and Anne of Brittany. At the foot of the sentry-walk are the back-to-back 'D's' of Diana of Poitiers; and under the porch, in mosaic, is the pattern of a wild boar, to remind us that Diana of Poitiers was also Diana the Huntress, partly from choice and partly because it enabled her to keep the goodwill of her father-in-law on the left hand, François I, and her almost-husband, Henri II, both passionately addicted to the chase. Of Catherine, there is no memento anywhere. Through the porch is the great courtyard and, thanks to the removal of the buildings of the north wing, already mentioned, there is a superb view from it over the terraces and down to the Loire, broad, sluggish and silvered here as everywhere along its length.

The Guard room is noteworthy for a painted ceiling (1559) on which are emblazoned the arms of Chaumont and

G

of Amboise; the paint can hardly have been dry when Catherine bought the château. There are two fine sixteenth-century Beauvais tapestries, depicting Hannibal's passage of the Alps and the Judgment of Paris. The only other room of particular interest that may be seen is Diana's reputed bedroom, in the right-hand entrance tower, giving into the Guard room. Here is an interesting portrait of Diana, a woman plain of face but showing great intelligence.

Here at Chaumont she spent the rest of her life; here she had the time that she had never had before to meditate upon the past. It was just thirty years since the death of her husband (one is tempted to say 'of her first husband', for her life with Henri was as perfectly domesticated as if they had been man and wife). He has a magnificent black-and-white marble tomb in Rouen cathedral. Always after his death she wore the black and white of the sorrowing widow, and the infatuated King adopted these as his own colours. There is a Latin epitaph engraved upon the tomb, in which the widow declares that 'as close as they had been in the nuptial chamber, so would they be in death', but the tomb was never opened to admit Diana's corpse to lie alongside this beloved husband. She was, in fact, buried in the chapel of her other lovely little château at Anet, the château that Henri had Philibert Delorme design for her.

Here she must have recaptured memories of her first meeting with Henri. François, to escape from captivity in Spain, agreed to hostages being taken in his place, and one of them was his son. Amongst the retinue of women accompanying this unattractive, wit-wandering child, was Diana.

It was François himself who, as his son approached manhood, chose his mistress for him. François had a high opinion of the common sense of Diana. There were reports, though not in the King's lifetime, that she had been his mistress first; but this is probably no more than calumny.

Whatever the truth of that may be, the King decided that it needed a woman of the intelligence and patience of Diana to make anything of his son, who was twenty years younger than she. The left-handed match was a brilliant success. Guided by Diana, the almost mentally-deficient Henri succeeded at least in holding his throne through times so troublesome that a much wiser man might well have lost his. Diana mothered him, nursed him, prompted him. She wore down eventually the sullen hatred of Catherine, his wife, and virtually took away from her even the management of the children of the marriage.

There seems to have been remarkably little romance in the accepted sense of the word about their connection, except perhaps during the young manhood of the Prince. They were the best of friends and companions; she was ever his guide and helper, from whom he could not bear to be separated. If all the subsequent French Kings' affairs with their mistresses had been as sexless as this, if the mistresses had been but one half as wise as Diana, French history might have taken a very different course.

Here in Chaumont the last six years must have passed slowly; no more Court painters now, to put on record an embellished record of her features; no sculptor of genius to make another statue of her as Diana the Huntress half-lying upon a stag, two hounds by her side, as in the masterpiece of Jean Goujon. (It is worth seeing it in the Louvre Museum, to where it was removed from Anet; her face and figure, judging from the portraits, have been greatly idealised.) Now over sixty, she was too old to ride to hounds again, too old to do more than live in the gilded past.

CHAPTER VII

Lion Couchant

(*AMBOISE*)

TO many misspent hours in the Montparnasse of the late 'twenties, I owe my inability to see Amboise from the river as anything else but a lion couchant heraldic above a formalised outline of roofs. Montparnasse was swarming with clever men and women who were making, or were about to make, their mark in the world of literature and the arts; but I have ever had an infinite capacity for loving lame ducks and none of my friends of the time have since come to the fore. It is, I suppose, a matter of sympathy; fond of music, I am incapable of playing or singing a note; interested in painting and drawing, I cannot make my fingers produce the line I can see so clearly in my mind's eye. It was inevitable that my heart should go out to the painters who could not paint, and the musicians who could not make music. At least they were very good company, which is more than could be said for some of the successful ones.

Amongst them was Tony, the son, I believe, of comfortably prosperous shopkeepers in England, who lived on a meagre allowance from home and drew terribly bad landscapes. Urged by his girl friend of the day, who had an eye for the commercial side of art, Tony went off to the Loire to earn some money by making drawings of the châteaux to sell to tourists. He came back, broke and enchanted. He had started at Amboise, fallen in love with it, and never moved from there until his money ran out. He made dozens and dozens of drawings of town and castle from every possible viewpoint, but the one that came up again and again was the castle seen from what used to be called the Ile d'Or, the Golden Island, and is now less romantically the Ile Saint-Jean. In each case the castle was recognisably an heraldic lion couchant; not until later did I realise that to obtain this effect he had taken certain artistic liberties, such as moving towers over to make the ears. These drawings might well have found a public amongst tourists were it not that by a strange misfortune the lionised castle bore an extremely strong resemblance to a Thurber dog. One result, as I have said, of Tony's month on the Loire was to make it impossible for me to see Amboise any other way than his; more serious in their effects on another member of our little fraternity were his drawings of the two towers, and that sad story will be told in its due place.

In fact, the château as seen from below has no well-defined shape; less than half of it remains, some of which is stern fortress, some late Gothic and some Renaissance domestic architecture; of the splendid gardens designed, like those of Blois, by Pacello there is nothing to be seen. Charles went to Italy and Italy captured his spirit. The Italian gardens, in particular, left him breathless. 'They need,' he wrote, 'but the presence of Adam and Eve to be the terrestrial paradise.' From thenceforth the garden became an integral part of the Renaissance château, but unhappily, of them all, only Villandry today can give us any conception of the all-important part the three-dimensional terraced garden played in the complete architectural scheme.

Amboise, however, is much older than the fifteenth century and is certainly the most ancient of all the châteaux of the Loire. Thanks to the Ile d'Or, the Loire could, from very early times, be spanned by two quite short bridges. Even before the first bridge, the relatively short distance from bank to island and from island to further bank made it an ideal place for troops to cross the river. The present castle stands on a little plateau commanding the passage, and some kind of camp has stood there from prehistoric days. Traces have been found of the Gallo-Roman fortress there; in the eleventh century it appears that there were two distinct forts on the plateau and one in the town, fighting against each other in family feuds and uniting only to repel some common enemy. Eventually town and forts passed into the possession of the Counts of Amboise, but not for long. Charles VII confiscated Amboise and made it the residence of the Queen, Charlotte of Savoy. There was born the Dauphin, later to be Charles VIII. The latter came to the throne at the early age of thirteen, and, though for some time in the leading-strings of his sister, soon showed a headstrong will of his own. The regency came to an end with his marriage to Anne of Brittany. In 1494, two years after he had begun the re-building of Amboise, he set off to conquer Italy, and wrote 'the first chapter in modern history'. The invasion became a triumphant procession, as Pisa was freed and Florence fell. Early in 1495 he occupied Naples: during this campaign, a new chapter in modern warfare was opened: the French artillery fired iron cannon-balls instead of the customary stone ones of the days of Joan of Arc. Venice, Spain, the Pope, Milan and the Emperor joined together against him and he had to retire.

He retired to Amboise with an enormous booty in furniture and textiles, in paintings and silverware. In his train came painters, sculptors, gardeners, tailors, artists and craftsmen (the two often indistinguishable) who were to transform the face of France.

He was to enjoy but two years of the arts of peace at Amboise. On the eve of Easter, 1498, a game of tennis was being played in the castle's defensive ditch. The opponents were well matched, the game exciting. Charles hurried off to fetch the Queen to see it. Returning, they had to pass through a low doorway in the outer wall; Charles, chatting happily with the Queen, forgot to bend, and hit his forehead hard against the lintel. For the moment he felt nothing, and continued to watch the game and talk with the Queen. Without warning, he fell backwards, senseless. The game was stopped, there was much shouting and calling and running to and fro, but nobody knew what to do. As he was so evidently dying, perhaps no courtier cared very much what happened to a moribund King. His body was placed in a stinking cellar, where he lay until eleven at night, when his breathing ceased.

In spite of the actual sites of these events having disappeared, the ghost of Charles VIII still haunts the castle; if you see a man, short and so broad as to appear misshapen, with an ugly yet not displeasing face, dressed in his late fifteenth-century costume of black velvet and cloth of gold, that will be the ghost of Charles; bow to him, please, because he was a King, and bow to him again because he brought to France, and through French influence to Britain, a more graceful way of life.

At Amboise, Charles VIII left the Logis du Roi, this Gothic building begun in 1491 before his Italian adventure (it is part of the frontage facing the Loire). It shows that the King's good taste was inborn, not entirely acquired from Italy. The gallery of the upper floor, under the roof, light and delicate; the rather fantastic dormer windows bristling with pinnacles like so many porcupines thrusting out their quills, are already signs of a mind breaking away from the Gothic discipline and searching for new forms.

The *Salle des Etats*, on the floor below, was the home in

exile of Abd-el-Kader, and cut up into apartments for him. This celebrated Arab Emir, born near Mascara about 1807, was for long a thorn in the side of the French. From 1832, he fought a fifteen-year battle against them and came close indeed to founding an Arab Empire of his own. After the capture of his own household by the cavalry of the Duc d'Aumale in 1843 and the defeat of his Moroccan allies the next year, his brilliant career as a soldier was over. He fought rear-guard actions for the next three years, surrendered, and was brought to France to be interned first at Toulon, then at the Château de Pau, and finally at Amboise. After long negotiations he was set free in 1853, and became thereafter a trusted and faithful friend of the French. His first view of a world newly freed to him was over the river at Amboise.

After this alteration to the *Salle des Etats* it remained rather derelict until, in 1906, it was entirely and on the whole successfully restored. Whether there is reasonable historical justification for the historiated capitals of the four columns, or whether the profusion of symbols, ermine and fleur-de-lys, represents an accurate reconstruction, I am doubtful. There is no doubt that the brick and stone construction, the double nave and vaulted ceiling, are faithful at least to the spirit of its earliest building. The windows give on to the Balcony of the Conspirators of evil fame, whose story belongs to a later period in this chapter.

Louis XII was the successor of Charles VIII; to consolidate the Crown he married the widowed Anne of Brittany. To him is due the foundation and ground floor of the Renaissance wing, completed by François I; three of the rooms are now furnished and hung with old tapestries to give some idea of their appearance at the time.

There was great jealousy between Blois and Amboise. At Blois there lived the provincial, plain and respectable Anne of Brittany (as mentioned above, the wing she might

one day have inhabited at Amboise was not finished in
her time), and life there was as dull as virtue could make it.
At Amboise, lived Louise of Savoy, 'urbane, exquisite and
immoral'.

To Amboise came little Fleurange, the tiny boy who had
travelled so far to place his sword and spear at the disposal
of Louis XII at Blois and whom the latter had sent on to
Amboise to be the playmate of Louise's son, Monsieur
d'Angoulême. Unless Louis XII had direct descendants,
which seemed very unlikely as long as he was married to
Anne of Brittany, Monsieur d'Angoulême was the heir-
apparent to the throne. His mother and his sister combined
in spoiling him, indulging his every whim. From the
moment that young François approved of this new companion, the ladies of the Court welcomed him with open
arms. The two boys played, and quarrelled, and played
again. 'Never,' wrote Fleurange in later years, 'was a
Prince who had more various pastimes than my Lord,'
and tells of 'leaping, tilting, bombarding mimic castles
and shooting with bow and arrow.' Unfortunately Fleurange, known as 'the adventurous youngster', was as little
gifted with ease of expression as are so many men of action,
and the record of his boyhood with the young King is as
stiff and dull as it ought to have been lively.

When, in 1514, Anne died at Blois, there was open rejoic-
ing at Amboise. The spoiled young François was now
certain to be King. Great plans were made for the future.

Then the revelry and the scheming at Amboise stopped
suddenly. Even the gay Louise 'grew pale and retired to
her own chamber' when the news was brought that the
fifty-two-year-old King was about to marry Mary Tudor,
sister of the English Henry VIII. She was only eighteen, and
there could be no doubt of her ability to bear sons and thereby put François' nose out of joint, and with it, indeed, the
noses of all the 'little court' at Amboise. There was no

reason to believe that the King was by any means too old
to become a father; and at scandal-loving Amboise there
was no lack of tongues to suggest that even if he were,
the Duke of Suffolk would take care that the new Queen
of France should bear an heir to the throne. Subsequent
events showed that the scandal-mongers had some grounds
for their malicious tittle-tattle.

At the beginning of October, Louis XII married his
young Princess, and Amboise settled down, ruefully, to a
much diminished importance. Then, in January, to the
undisguised joy of Louise and her family, Louis died. But
Louis had left a widow, and that widow might still bear
him a posthumous son who would be King of France.
Fearful and complicated were the intrigues that followed.
Mary Tudor was young and as headstrong as her brother.
Encouraged in her own desire by the whole of the supporters of the Amboise clan, impatient in her youth, she waited
only for the minimum six weeks of mourning, and then
married Charles Brandon, Duke of Suffolk (who had come
in her train), and returned to England. Monsieur d'Angoulême had become H.M. François I. The great days of Amboise had begun.

Oddly enough you enter the fortress of Amboise now by
taking the Rue de la Concorde, which is not what one would
have expected from its previous history. Certainly this
part of the little town is made delightful by a handful of
Renaissance houses, carved and corbelled, and wonder-
fully aslant. Then you come to a vaulted passage, and this
brings you into what used to be the courtyard of the castle.
You must imagine it in the times of François as entirely
surrounded by buildings, on whose grey walls were no
fewer than 4,000 hooks to hang the tapestries for the many
fêtes that were given there.

Overhead, on wet days, a canopy would be raised, golden
sun and moon and stars on a blue background. Almost

any occasion would bring the court into use. There was for example the midnight wedding of Duke Urbino, which was 'marvellously triumphant, with all the dancing and ballets possible.' The minstrels were accompanied by 72 damsels 'disguised as Germans and Italians' who beat time with their tambourines. Such was the number of torches, that 'when dawn came, none noticed that the light was any stronger.' A wedding, a victory, the visit of a friendly Prince, or just the plain desire to be gay, were reasons enough for a fête and when the young King, who was only twenty-one, had had enough of music and poetry and singing, which was seldom, then the courtyard was turned into a miniature battle-ground for the exercise of arms, or lions or wild boars or mastiffs were let loose for the men to show their courage and their skill at arms. The story is told of the wild boar that escaped one day from the courtyard, forced its way through a door into the palace proper and spread alarm and despondency as it went. François, the hunter (you will remember how his departure for the chase immediately after his wedding to the unhappy Claude, daughter of Anne of Brittany by her first husband, was described in the chapter on Blois), was ready for it. All his gallant gentlemen were outside, and the more they shouted and tried to get at the boar from behind, the more they drove the animal into the palace and added to its fright and fury. François drew his sword, side-stepped the forward onrush, and despatched the animal with a single thrust between the shoulder blades, to the admiring shrieks of the ladies and the ecstatic praise of the courtiers.

The setting for these fêtes was often most elaborate. François had almost a mania for 'hydraulic devices', and a schoolboy's sense of humour. Delicately wrought, temporary fountains would be erected, and when the richly-dressed crowd gathered round to admire, as the fountain was set working, the King would give a signal and the jet of water would change direction and soak the onlookers. It may have been difficult, but it was essential for all who desired to remain in favour at Court, to laugh as heartily as the King at a misadventure which cost the victim the price of a rich velvet suit, and possibly a good head-cold into the bargain.

It must, I think, have been some such episode as this, with some richly amoral ending, that fat Joseph set about telling a few years before his death. A little party had emerged from the vaulted passage on to what is now the terrace and was once the courtyard. There was the English lady, unbearably superior; there was her daughter, exceedingly pretty (you may have noticed how the most unlikely parents always have the prettiest daughters); there was a dark young man who had made their acquaintance at the little hotel that is one of the joys of Amboise and who was very much taken with the pretty daughter. The daughter had made it clear that she had a distinct inclination towards the dark young man. In the setting of the romantic castles of the Loire, the end of the story seemed, up to the meeting with Joseph, inevitable.

Joseph was not an official guide, but turned an honest penny by attaching himself to visitors who were waiting for one. He was fat and cheerful, loquacious and apparently well-informed. Few cold-shouldered him, or refused him a few francs when they left. Few knew, or cared, whether the stories he told of Amboise were truth or invention; they were always good stories, well told.

The two ladies strolled over to admire the view from the terrace. The young man was about to follow them when Joseph button-holed him and asked him if he knew the funniest story about this terrace that used to be a courtyard. Unless the young man had taken to his heels and bolted, he could not have got away from the expert Joseph, who started, with much gesticulation, to tell his story. Un-

fortunately, it was after lunch, and Joseph had drunk deep
of the heady wine of Chinon. Not a single comprehensible
sentence had he uttered before the excellent humour of his
own story hit him amidships; he laughed out loud, with
a great infectious belly laugh; he laughed until the tears
streamed down his face; he laughed until he was incapable
of uttering a single word, intelligible or not. He was
irresistible; the young man began to laugh at Joseph, and
that made Joseph laugh the more; until the sight of him,
with mouth wide open exhaling fumes like an open tun of
wine, with hands on sides trying in vain to control the
huge heavings of his great belly, reduced the young man
to a state of hilarious incapacity.

At this moment the ladies came hurrying up to share in
the joke, mother with a forced but would-be graceful
smile, until she got the full blast of Joseph's vinous breath,
when she reared up and fell back like a startled mare.
'May we,' she said in her most County voice, 'May we be
allowed to share the joke?'

The young man, between sobs of laughter, tried to make
her understand that there wasn't one, yet, but that Joseph
would doubtless tell it to them all. With a glance at the
poor young man that would have sent the basilisk green
with envy, the mother turned away, calling to her daughter,
'Helen, this is clearly a smoking-room tale. We will leave
the men to enjoy it. *I* have never been interested in *that*
kind of story.' Helen followed her mother, but turned
round to indicate by rapid signs to the young man that
she sympathised with him and was quite ready to be made
a fellow-conspirator.

The guide appeared; the ladies started to go with him
towards the Saint Hubert Chapel. The somewhat sobered
Joseph now found that too much laughter had had a
physical effect on him, and turned to do that little service
to nature which is more often done against a convenient

wall in France than in the Anglo-Saxon countries. He was
in full view of the mother as she gave a last disapproving
glance round to see if the young man had forsaken his
disreputable acquaintance and could be permitted to join
her again after due apology. The sight that met her eyes
froze her face into a passable imitation of one of M. Viollet-
le-Duc's gargoyles on Notre-Dame, and the young man
understood that he had better delay any attempt at a
rapprochement.

They did not meet again until the evening; the hotel was
too small for them not to. Mother was distinctly cold,
daughter brimming over with anticipation. It was not
until long after dinner that the mother left them alone for a
few minutes. 'Quick, before she comes back again, what
was that dirty story the funny old man was telling you?'
In vain the poor young man explained that there just
hadn't been one. Even to himself, he failed to sound con-
vincing.

'You are a pig,' said Helen, inelegantly. 'You know I
won't repeat it to mother. She'd never understand, but
you might at least tell me.'

Desperately the young man tried to convince her that
he had been laughing at nothing, that he didn't know why
he was laughing, that if he did know, there was nothing
that would give him greater pleasure than to tell her; but
the more he protested, the more Helen was certain he was
holding out on her. 'You think I'm too young to hear it,
don't you? Well I'm not. At school we knew lots of stories
much worse than anything that old man could tell you.
Quick now, mother will be back at any moment. If you
don't tell me, I swear I'll never speak to such a spoil-sport
again.'

The young man couldn't tell her. Helen had inherited a
good deal of her mother's determination, and kept her
word. Next day they parted with cold politeness on both

sides, and a most promising romance came to an abrupt
end through a funny story that was never told. And when,
some years later, the young man visited Amboise again,
Joseph had gone the way of all flesh. The only consolation
left to the young man was the thought that Helen might
have taken after her mother in the years to come.

The view from what is now the terrace is a noble one:
over the Ile d'Or where once the Visigoth Alaric and the
Frankish Clovis signed a treaty, over the town whose
buildings span so many centuries, out to the little manor
house, the Clos Lucé, where Leonardo da Vinci lived his
last few years and where he died, gazing at his own
Giaconda.

François had been King for only a year when he persuaded
the greatest genius of the Renaissance to come and live in
Touraine. What artistic work he did here is not very clear;
certainly he designed the murals of the oratory, but they
have been ruined by heavy-handed and uninspired restoration. His ever-active brain was busy with a thousand schemes
for François that had little to do with the arts. A canal
through the centre of France; some of those hydraulic
works which François adored, schemes for protecting
armies during the crossing of rivers, and something closely
resembling the submarine. The light-hearted King loved
Leonardo, but paid no attention to the schemes that were
submitted. In three years Leonardo was dead and was
buried in the collegiate church of Saint Florentin, below
the castle. His presumed skeleton was discovered in 1869,
and buried anew in the Saint Hubert Chapel in 1874, but the
evidence regarding the origin of these bones is unsatisfactory.

From the terrace this chapel of Saint Hubert is the first
part of the castle the guide takes you to visit. Much as
I usually dislike writing of the 'best' or the 'worst' of anything, in this case I feel justified in saying that the most perfect building the final phase of French Gothic has left us

is this tiny chapel. It was completed in 1493; the Renaissance was already knocking on the door to come in. It has none of the soaring majesty of the Gothic cathedrals; it is, in fact, a single specimen, unique in its beauty.

The front faces the gardens, and the apse, for some reason excellent at the time doubtless but quite incomprehensible now, projects over the rampart and is supported by a massive buttress, so that the chapel is astride the outer wall. It is remarkable that it has survived the passage of time, but more remarkable still that it did not collapse when a shell exploded on a main crossbeam in 1940. It survived further damage in 1944.

Outside, the lintel is graced by a most beautiful carving in high relief of, on the left, Saint Christopher bearing the Child Christ (alas, a shell-burst obliterated the Child's head), and, on the right, the Vision of Saint Hubert, in which the saint saw a cross appear miraculously between the antlers of a stag. Above, on the tympanum, the Virgin appears between Charles VIII and Anne of Brittany. So perfect is this work that there has long been debate as to its origin. No French artists of the time, so far as is known, could have been responsible for sculpture of such delicacy and feeling. On the other hand, it bears no relation to the Italianate work that was so soon to succeed it. The general opinion seems to be that Charles (who, as mentioned above, was gifted with natural good taste) brought Flemish artists to decorate his favourite chapel.

The interior is no less rich, with beautifully worked vaults and arches; but the guide always hurries the visitors through before they have time to study its interesting details. People in the mass, and particularly holiday crowds, seem to be such vandals that it is, I suppose, impossible to let them loose over places such as Amboise; but the haste of guides in general to whip their little crowds in and out again deprives those genuinely interested of much pleasure.

9. CHENONCEAU. *The gallery:* 'Philibert Delorme, faced with the difficulty of adding to an already nearly perfect building, produced a masterpiece differing from, yet marrying happily with, the main body of the château.'

10. VALENÇAY. '*The château is unique; it is a monument of the decadence of Renaissance art.*'

After the death of Leonardo da Vinci, François came but seldom to Amboise. The last notable record of his visits there is in 1539, when he received the Emperor Charles V in full state. He chose to receive him in the Tour des Minimes, a part of the château so remarkable that Charles could never have seen its like before. He ended by praying that he might never see it again.

The Tour des Minimes is a round tower something over 68 feet in diameter, and served as a means of access to the castle from the river side. Round a central pillar is a winding ramp, supported by ogival arches, carefully graduated so that a horseman may ride up it. In Renaissance days you might have seen the astonishing sight of a massive fortress tower of considerable height, with horsemen emerging from near the top of it. The ramp is wide enough to justify the claim that sledges, horse-drawn, bearing provisions and munitions, could use it. This was certainly true of the other tower, the slightly wider Tour Hurtault.

To receive Charles, the whole of the inside of the tower was covered in tapestries. An army of torch-bearers lined the ramp. When Charles was half-way up, one of the torches set fire to the hangings and in a few minutes the whole tower was filled with smoke. Some tried to push the Emperor's horse upwards towards the exit and the fresh air, others were trying to lead it down again, as being quicker than going up, and the horse itself, choking and blinded by the smoke, just refused to move at all. Finally, the burning tapestry was pulled down and stamped on until the smouldering was finished, buckets of water were passed down to extinguish any sparks that might be setting fire to others, and the Emperor, more than half-asphyxiated and still not quite certain that no attempt on his life was intended, came out into the cold night air at the higher level.

Amongst the drawings that young Tony, mentioned at the beginning of this chapter, brought back from Amboise

H

were a number of both the Tour des Minimes and its companion piece, the Tour Hurtault. However bad they were, the purpose of the ramp was made very plain. These drawings gave rise to great argument.

Another of our little group was a very large Texan, Charles, who had been brought up with horses, had lived horses and talked horses all his life until, in a moment of complete madness, he decided to come to Paris to paint. I think perhaps that, a generation later, he might have been taken up during the recent search for living 'primitives' and made a success of his painting. As it was, his huge pictures found no market, and Charles idled away his time and drank far too much. When he drank, his talk was always of horses, and what he could do with them, which was everything except make them talk back to him.

His argument, on seeing the Tour des Minimes drawings, was that such a ramp was totally unnecessary; he would undertake to get any horse up any flight of stairs, including the Eiffel Tower. We pounced on him, and asked how he proposed to get the horse down again. Anybody, we claimed (though none of us would have cared to have tried) could get a horse up, but no power on earth would persuade a horse to turn round and come down again. 'You leave it to me,' was all that Charles said, and the conversation turned to other matters.

I had forgotten all about this argument when I learned to my astonishment some days later that Charles was to appear in a Magistrate's Court. I was amazed, for even in drink Charles was the gentlest man of his size alive, and at all times honest as could be. The case against him, it appeared, was of having stolen a horse. The story, with some difficulty, I pieced together afterwards.

After an all-night sitting at the Dôme, Charles was on his way home, not perhaps entirely sober. At the corner of his street he met a milk cart, horse-drawn. All unattended horses, according to him, were lonely. He took pity on the poor neglected creature, removed it from the shafts and proceeded with it towards his own little flat. Then the argument of those few days before came back to him, and he decided it was a heaven-sent opportunity to show us what he could do.

How he persuaded that horse up the narrow staircase of a Montparnasse tenement building we shall never know. It was not done without a certain amount of noise. Sleepy but indignant heads peeped out of flat doors on the first, the second, the third and then the fourth floors. That was as far as he got with the horse before the shrieks from the same sleepy but indignant heads woke the concierge. The sight, as he climbed up towards the noise, of the large posterior of a horse sent him clattering down again and out into the street to fetch a bewildered policeman who was quite convinced that a barely-clothed man babbling to him at five in the morning about a horse stuck on the staircase four floors up must of necessity be drunk. It took them all day to get the horse down again, step by step, backwards, Charles refusing to help and sulking in his own flat until the police came to arrest him.

He paid heavy costs (fortunately he was by far the wealthiest of us) and put on suspended sentence. We were not to have his company for much longer. A second unfortunate episode with a horse, removed this time in the dead of night from one of the fast-disappearing horse-cabs, both because it looked lonely and because Charles felt he would die if he did not ride a horse again, ended in his being arrested whilst riding bare-backed in the Bois de Boulogne. He again received a suspended sentence, but this time only on condition that he left France.

After the misadventure of Charles V, there remains but one outstanding event in the history of the castle, the Conspiracy of Amboise in 1560.

There is no need to go into great detail of its origin. It was during the height of the religious troubles. Catherine de Médicis was at Amboise with the boy King, François II, and his girl wife, Mary, Queen of Scots to be. Far away in Brittany, a Protestant gentleman, one La Renaudie, formulated a plan by which the conspirators should take possession of the young King at Amboise and carry him off to Blois, where he would be persuaded to grant them the right to practise their religion. The plot was betrayed to the Guise family. The Court left Amboise, and took refuge in Blois, which was the more easily defended.

Of this the conspirators knew nothing and, arriving at Amboise in small groups, were taken by the Guise faction. Some were killed on the spot; the leaders were tortured. When it was considered safe, when all the conspirators had arrived at Amboise and been accounted for, the royal family returned.

Some of the conspirators were hanged from the balcony now known as the *Balcon des Conjurés*, some from the battlements, some thrown alive into the Loire in sacks, some broken on the wheel. The carnage went on for several days, and the horrible story goes on that the royal family, after dinner, came out 'in spite of the stench of decaying corpses, to see the grimaces and contortions of those that were still hanging alive from the battlements.' This is not authenticated beyond all possibility of doubt and has been much publicised by the Protestants and attacked by the Catholics; one can only say that it may be true and that the probabilities are in favour of its being so.

Yet it is difficult to reconcile all that we know of the gay and gracious young Queen Mary at this time with this form of *divertissement*. Perhaps the only truly happy times she ever knew were in her girlhood at the French Court. Though betrothed to François at eight years of age, she was allowed to reach the maturity of sixteen before the marriage to this delicate boy took place. She had already made her reputation for 'her beauty, her good manners and her appetite.' To Paris, in her girlhood, she brought a new fashion which all the great ladies followed, the *escoffion*, or little bonnet worn right on the back of the head, which showed off her girlish good looks to perfection.

The young François adored her and obeyed her in everything, this gay little creature who loved nothing better than to dance and to sing and to be surrounded by happy faces. Her mother-in-law fell equally under her charm; 'she has but to appear,' she wrote, 'for all French heads to be turned.' Indeed, in later years she did all she could to reconcile Mary to Elizabeth. When George Buchanan, a Scot permanently resident in Paris and much appreciated by the Pleiad, turned against the young Queen he had previously praised, and wrote against her a terrible diatribe, *De Maria Scotorum Regina*, Catherine had the book publicly burned and commissioned Belleforest to prepare an answer, *L'Innocence de Madame Marie*.

When the young King died so soon after the marriage, Mary was 'in great dolour'. Brantôme describes her in her mourning, 'the white mourning which became her so well, for the pallor of her face vied with the whiteness of her veil as to which would be the more colourless, but the artificial whiteness of the cloth could not contend with the snow-whiteness of her visage.'

When she left France, weeping, crying out, 'Adieu, France. Adieu, France,' her little brother-in-law, the new King Charles IX, tried to console her and regretted only, he said, 'that I am too young to marry you myself.'

She was a lover of poetry, too, this young girl. 'I have seen her read fine poems and elegies,' wrote Brantôme, 'both in France and in Scotland, that brought tears to her eyes and sighs to her heart.'

Is this gay, yet sensitive, young girl, this lovable, feminine creature, the one who went outside after dinner to take pleasure in the cries and the grimaces of dying men, Protestants and traitors though they were? It seems difficult to believe, yet life in the Renaissance was contradictory in the extreme. Supremely civilised people were guilty of excesses of cruelty that were normal at the time but which would turn us sick now, were it not that we have seen what Continental dictatorships have done to make the cruellest men of the Renaissance seem almost angels by comparison.

A short walk, less than half a mile, takes one to the very different atmosphere of the Clos Lucé, a Renaissance manor house of rose-red brick framed in square-cut white stone, with a sharply pointed slated roof and a single rectangular watch-turret. Here, on May 2, 1519, died that universal genius, Leonardo da Vinci. It is now open to the public every day, and the visit to this peaceful and charming residence is well worth while. The bedroom in which he died is most evocative, and in the recently opened chapel are frescoes which, at least in part, he may well have painted himself. An angel leading the heavenly choir most certainly owes its inspiration to him.

In this delightful house he spent much of his time on imaginative drawings. It is difficult not to believe that the oriental splendour of the skyline of Chambord, described in the final chapter, does not derive from the King's familiarity with the artist's doodlings of Eastern domes and minarets, or that the spirals of the shells that it was his delight to draw were not the first rough outlines of the majestic staircases at Blois and Chambord.

Francesco Melzi, the devoted companion and follower of Leonardo, broke the news of his death to the latter's brothers, and wrote as noble an epitaph as any man could desire: 'the loss of such a man must be mourned by all and it is not within the power of nature to create another like him'.

CHAPTER VIII

The White Lady

(CHANTELOUP AND CHENONCEAU)

THE great forest stretches for miles around Amboise and in it are many beautiful and some strange things to see. The queerest, and in its own peculiar way not the least beautiful, is Chanteloup.

It lies only two miles from the château of Amboise, at the entrance of the forest. It is one huge joke.

The château of Chanteloup was built during the childhood of Louis XV for Jean d'Aubigny. It was later bought and greatly enlarged by Choiseul during the time he was the powerful Minister of Louis XV, who had already presented him with Amboise.

He was honest enough, or careless enough, to fall foul of Madame du Barry. In time she influenced the King sufficiently to have Choiseul rusticated to his domain of Chanteloup for an indefinite period which, in fact, lasted four years. Choiseul was not the man to take exile lying down. From 1770 until the King's death in 1774 he held a Court at Chanteloup to rival that of Louis XV himself. As a disgraced Minister he was powerful enough still to attract the most notable men of his day, who risked the King's anger in coming to see him.

When his exile was over, Choiseul did not forget those who remained his friends during the days of his disgrace. In their memory he had built, in the taste of the times for

Chinoiseries, a pagoda. Le Camus was ordered to take as model the pagoda built in Kew Gardens in 1762. Like his master, Le Camus saw things in a big way. It took from 1775 to 1778 to complete it; but when he had done, he had transformed the stocky Kew Garden pagoda into something enormously bigger, incomparably lighter in appearance and more elegant in style. The six floors, diminishing as they rise, make a rough pyramid, of which the apex is about 125 feet high; they stand on a circular peristyle 50 feet in diameter, composed of sixteen columns and sixteen pillars.

It was, in other words, something comparable to the English Folly, a fragile and temporary decoration to the vast and massive château. Part of the joke of Chanteloup is that the solid château has utterly disappeared (all but two small courtyard pavilions), and the evanescent Folly alone remains.

As you come along the Route de Bléré from Amboise you pass on your left the cemetery in which this Duc de Choiseul lies buried (he died, perhaps happily for him, before the Revolution, in 1785); a little beyond, to the right, is the forest ride leading to the pagoda. As you approach, the other part of the joke, the conscious joke that Le Camus played, becomes apparent. The outline at first seems Chinese enough, or at least more Chinese than Brighton's Pavilion is Indian; then the eye picks out the peristyle, the very essence of the neo-classicism of the time, 'the grace of Versailles bearing aloft the time-honoured silhouette of the far distant Cathay.'

It is difficult to believe that Le Camus did not design this building with his tongue as far in his cheek as he could put it without disaster, combining in one building the two fads of the day, the classical and the Chinese, so as to please everybody. It is a parody of the current taste which led to the classically-proportioned rooms of the new palaces being

made alive with lacquered monkeys and other supposedly
Chinese designs. Le Camus surpassed them all, carrying
this Sino-classical incongruity into the very structure and
outer appearance of his Folly.

Against the theory that Le Camus suffered from an over-
developed sense of humour, one must record the other
supposition that Le Camus, tiring of perpetually contradictory instructions from the dictatorial Duke, who vacillated
between a bigger and better Kew pagoda, and a classical
building, developed in height from a Grecian temple,
combined both ideas in a single unit and resolved the
Duke's doubts with this unexpected master-stroke.

However it happened, there it is; the only pagoda in the
world with a colonnade, four wrought-iron balconies and
Louis XVI style decoration throughout. Outside, above
the European-style ground-floor windows, are Chinese
characters engraved on black stones, claimed to signify
Knowledge, Goodness and Concord, but, never having
had the opportunity of visiting it with a native of China,
I have no means of knowing if the 'Chinese' characters are
not as fake as the rest.

Each floor consists of a circular room, domed, reached
by an inner staircase ornamented by a wrought-iron rail
in which the letter 'C' is repeatedly interwoven in the design.
On the first floor, it is said, the marble tables once bore the
names of all those friends of Choiseul who came to visit
him during his exile; for their safety, it is claimed, the tables
were reversed when the Revolution came, lest they provide
an all too handy list of *ci-devants* to proscribe.

From the top of the pagoda, 500 feet above sea level,
the whole valley of the Loire from Blois to Tours, can be
seen in one single and magnificent panoramic sweep, with
countless woods and forests fringing the distant horizon.

Through the forest, half woods, half heath, the road
leads first to Bléré, where we first meet the Cher and then,

almost immediately, to what is probably the best-known and possibly the most beautiful of all the Loire châteaux, Chenonceau. (There is much confusion regarding this name, even amongst the French themselves; for the sake of convenience I have adopted the point of view of those who claim that as a place-name it is Chenonceaux, and as the name of a particular building, Chenonceau. Whether this is 'right' and other opinions 'wrong' it is as useless to argue as it is to discuss which is the 'right' spelling of Shakespeare's name when he himself could not make up his own mind.)

I had intended at first to write little about it. It is familiar already to so many from actual visits, from drawings, paintings and photographs, that I felt there could be nothing new to say about its architecture and its history. I found that to be true enough, and yet at the same time discovered in casual conversations here and there that there was more misunderstanding of both than I had believed possible. I hope that those who know Chenonceau will be content enough to have their memory stirred, and that those who believe that the much-photographed gallery across the river is all that matters of its architecture and that its possession for a dozen years by Diana of Poitiers is the one important fact of its history, will find hereafter good reasons to change their opinions.

To begin with the château as one sees it now: the approach is up a long and dusty drive edged by enormous plane trees, leading to a forecourt. This is guarded by a brace of sphinxes, to the right of which are outbuildings. Amongst these are the stables, designed by Philibert Delorme in 1560, pleasing enough, but not particularly interesting.

From here the first view of the château comes upon you with all the shock of surprise, if you are one of those who are familiar with it only from the printed page; you

find yourself looking upon something completely unexpected for, from the front, neither the great gallery across
the river nor the river itself are visible. Instead there is a
decorative drawbridge leading to the rectangular terrace,
surrounded by a moat, that marks the site of the original
château. There, too, is a splendid, stalwart cylindrical
keep, dating from feudal times and somewhat refashioned
later in the taste of the Renaissance, which no photograph
has shown you as dominating Chenonceau. Two decorative
and very formal gardens stretch right and left along the
bank of the still invisible Cher. Behind drawbridge and
keep, a bridge leads to the château proper, built upon the
twin bank-abutments of an antique mill linked by a narrow
arch.

It is a tremendous moment, this; expecting something so
familiar as to have become almost hackneyed, one discovers
instead a completely unsuspected gem in stone-work, for
of that well-known gallery there is still no sign. The great
steep-pitched roof (half as high again, incidentally, as the
roof of the gallery), with huge and superbly ornamented
dormer windows and, above them, daring chimney-
groups used to perfect the scheme of decoration; at the
four corners of the square-built main block are exquisite
turrets, so perfect in proportion that one feels that an inch
less or an inch more in diameter would have ruined them,
surmounted by conical turrets, and ending above ground
level on gracefully graduated round brackets. It is impossible to convey in words the *rightness* of everything; you
may look at it for hours, mentally adding and taking away,
and at the end you will find that there is nothing you
could change to advantage. It does not even err from over-
uniformity, for upstream on the eastern side a tiny chapel
and a matching wing protrude to frame, at ground level,
a little terrace that relieves it from all danger of monotony.
This is, indeed, of all the châteaux of the Loire, the 'maiden

most perfect, lady of light', utterly feminine in character, without weakness yet without a single concession to troublous times, beyond the domesticated keep (complete with tall Renaissance chimney) and the ornamental draw-bridge.

To see the famous gallery, it is necessary to turn into one or other of the gardens as far as the Cher. There it will be seen that it is an extension (and a later addition) to the southern façade. Philibert Delorme, faced with the diffi-culty of adding to an already nearly perfect building, produced a masterpiece, differing from, yet marrying hap-pily with, the main body of the château. It is about 200 feet long, crossing the full width of the Cher on five arches, ending on cutwaters, each of which carries a semicircular turret rising to the height of the beginning of the second floor. Above this second floor, the long roof-line is broken on each side by nine small dormers. At each end of the roof is a tall, rectangular chimney. The gallery is, in fact, un-finished on the southern bank, where it was intended to link up with a square tower which was to be an additional entrance; its absence is not obvious and does not detract from the appearance of the château as seen from either side.

Such is Chenonceau, the 'White Lady of Touraine'. It carries an air of complete serenity. Yet its history has been connected with events so greatly at variance with its beauty, its dignity and its air of restfulness that one learns of its past with something of the same shock that comes when one discovers that a beautiful and gracious woman, with an unlined and untroubled face, has been the leading character in some ignoble scandal.

Some time during the Hundred Years War, the fortress then existing at Chenonceaux was burnt or otherwise destroyed. The ground belonged to Jean Marques, amongst whose titles was that of Seigneur de Chenonceaux. In

1432, he petitioned Charles VII for permission to rebuild it,
which was duly granted. A new keep arose and, at the same
time, a fortified mill was built on the bank of the Cher.
One of the most valuable of feudal rights, maintained until
the Revolution, was that of insisting that all corn from the
region should be ground at the Seigneur's mill. At Chenonceaux, the mill paid for the fort, and the fort protected the
mill.

In spite of the value of the mill, the Marques family
spent more money than they received (one suspects there
may have been here, as was fairly general in France, a good
deal of 'black market' milling). Piece by piece, the plots of
land around were sold. Very quietly, through nominees,
they were purchased by one Thomas Bohier. He was a
banker, a man of no social distinction, and owing his situation in life to his own efforts and to his marriage into the
de Semblançay family, powerful financiers. He became
Receiver-General of Finances; it would appear that not all
he received found its way into the King's coffers. Either he
or, much more probably, his wife Katherine Briçonnet,
fell in love with the site and determined to possess it.
Katherine was a native of these parts, and presumably
familiar with it.

His purchases went quietly on, until the day came when
the Marques family could not enter their own keep without
passing through Bohier's property. In 1496 he claimed also
to have purchased keep and mill, but the Marques family,
through one of the longest and most complicated law suits
of the time, fought a legal rear-guard action against dispossession which ended only in 1512. The final purchase
price was 12,500 livres, but the lawyers' fees must have
brought it to many times that figure.

Within a year of entering into final possession, masons
were already at work knocking down the old and laying
the foundations of the new. Bohier, the servant of François I,

left to serve his master in Italy. The new château was built to the order and under the direction of Katherine.

Of its strongly feminine character externally, I have already written; internally, the design of a woman of taste and common sense is equally evident. She broke away from tradition; the labyrinthine sequence of room and ante-room, one giving into the other *ad infinitum*, was done away with. Instead, there was a central hall with four large rooms giving off it, to make service the easier. Instead of the inevitable spiral staircase, a straight stairway led to the upper floor. Katherine was obviously a woman of great strength of character to break away from tradition in this manner, and it must not be forgotten that, whether or not the building on the piles of the demolished mill was her inspiration, the responsibility for the decision lay with her.

Perhaps because of its novelty, the building of the château dragged on until 1521. Masons are no less conserv-ative and traditional in their outlook than any other crafts-men, and the master-mason of the times, architect, artist and artisan all in one, was a power to be reckoned with. Katherine must have had many a wordy battle with the men, set in their ways and not welcoming innovations, before she got her own way. As far as I can trace, Chenonceau was a carry-over from the Middle Ages in that it was not form-ally designed by an architect.

Three years later, Bohier died in the Milanese. He had seen little of his wife's dream house, which she herself had occupied for only five years when death came mercifully upon her to spare her the knowledge of the tragic end of Jacques de Semblançay, the principal member of her family, and the dispossession of the Bohier dynasty.

Of the gay and cheerfully immoral Louise de Savoie, something has already been said in the previous chapter. Entertaining companion as she may have been, she shared with many other women of dubious morals a total lack of scruples in acquiring money. During François' frequent absences in Italy, she had a good deal to say in affairs of state.

In 1522, the year after Chenonceau was completed, Jacques de Semblançay, the King's Treasurer and Katherine's distinguished relative, was ordered to send a large sum of money to Lautrec in Italy. Lautrec proceeded to lose the Milanese, giving as the principal reason that no funds had reached him. At once de Semblançay disclaimed all fault in the matter, and completely convinced Lautrec of his innocence. Thereupon both Lautrec and the Constable Bourbon attacked Louise de Savoie as the cause of the disaster.

François, for all his façade of jollity, was a mean and revengeful man. An attack upon his mother he considered as an attack upon himself, although he must have known full well of what she was capable in her passion for accumulating money. He instituted a Commission for the examination of the Treasurer's books. His captivity in Spain in 1525 and 1526 put a stop to the Commission's work; but the case was re-opened, in 1527, after Francois' return and a year after Katherine's death.

A trial that was a complete mockery of justice followed. In spite of his years (he was eighty-two, an age seldom attained at that time) and a reputation for integrity rare indeed in that or the subsequent three reigns, de Semblançay was condemned for corruption. To the King's eternal shame the death penalty was invoked.

Clément Marot, the rhymer of the Psalms, the poet of the dubious past, records public opinion on the execution in some rather indifferent verse. 'Hell,' in the context, is the Paris Châtelet, whose rigours Marot himself had tasted and of which he had written in a previous poem, *L'Enfer*. 'Montfaulcon' was the criminals' place of execution.

'When Maillart,' he wrote, 'Judge of Hell, was taking Samblançay to Montfaulcon to render up his soul, which of the two, do you imagine, carried himself the better? Let me tell you; Maillart seemed the man about to die, and Samblançay such a stalwart old man that anybody would have thought he was taking Lieutenant Maillart to Montfaulcon.'

Louise died four years later. Like the Medici, she was a profound believer in astrology. She sat up all through a cold night to study a comet and calculate its presages, caught a chill, and died, to the grief of few beyond the King. She left a fortune of a million and a half gold coins, a sum that must have made her the richest woman in France. How much of this was the money for which de Semblançay went to the scaffold we can never know; but the mere size of this enormous fortune, added to the Treasurer's reputation for integrity, gives enormous weight to the evidence he produced at his trial that Louise had, by the authority of her position, ordered him to hand over to her the sum destined for Lautrec, with the assurance that she would ensure its transport to Italy. To all this evidence, Louise returned a flat denial. The word of the King's mother won the day, as we have seen, in a packed trial.

The vengeful François was not satisfied that the family had yet paid dearly enough for de Semblançay's hardihood in accusing Louise. There still remained young Bohier at Chenonceau, related to them through his mother. He must pay, and pay through the nose.

The elder Bohier had died years before, in the King's service. No matter, the old books must be checked. There was none to defend Bohier; if there had been, it would have made no difference to the King who had learned from his mother how both to spend your gold and have it. The accounts were audited; enormous sums were found, genuinely or otherwise, to be missing. Young Antoine Bohier paid until he was stripped of everything. Finally, in 1535, Chenonceau passed to François, and the ruined Antoine was left in poverty, and peace.

11. MONTRESOR. 'The double surrounding walls are in part cut into the rock mass on which it is built . . . it is practically impossible to determine what is natural and what is artificial.'

12. LOCHES. '. . . *the enchanting Renaissance Town Hall which leans, almost literally, against the fifteenth-century town gate (Porte Picoys).*'

13. LOCHES. . . . *seen from the River Indre, 'the towers, the turrets, the roofs, the pinions, the little houses and the enormous castle . . . pressed in together.'*

14. Azay-le-Rideau. 'In its design it incorporates the features of the fortified castle of the Middle Ages, attenuated into the purely decorative.'

Having cast envious eyes upon another's toy, child-like, François made no use of it when he had taken it. Chenonceau stood unoccupied for years, with the King coming very occasionally for hunting. It was on one of these occasions that two future owners of the château saw it for the first time.

Ten years after François had taken possession, he arrived at Chenonceau with a large party. Amongst them were his unloved son, his son's wife and his son's mistress. Diana of Poitiers saw Chenonceau, and remembered it. Catherine de Médicis saw it, and also remembered it. It must have looked very lovely in all its unselfconscious beauty against a background of trees just bursting into leaf, its new, clean stone showing to perfection against the light blue sky and delicate green. The self-assured Diana, the calculating, patient, far-seeing Catherine, had become once more rivals in their desires.

Just two years later, François died in the spring of 1547; the Dauphin became Henri II; Catherine de Médicis became Queen; Diana became the new owner of Chenonceau.

In all but name, Diana had in fact become Queen. The doting King, twenty years her junior, could do nothing without the mistress his father had chosen for him with such worldly wisdom. It reminds me, every time I think of it, of an episode of a quarter of a century ago, when the father of a French lad with whom I was friendly, explained to me at some length that he had chosen his son's first mistress for him, for safety's sake. 'A good, sound, reliable woman of forty, who'd been my own mistress years ago. I knew I could have every confidence in her.' He was distressed to hear that my father was not doing as much for me. There are times when the Channel separates two very different worlds.

In the case of François, as I have already mentioned, the

I

evidence that Diana had ever been his mistress is no more than one rumour circulating in a scandal-mongering Court where a new one was invented every day, but his reputation was such that every woman he noticed was immediately suspected of having slept with him.

At first money was lacking to do all she wished to do with this much desired present she had received from the King. It was nine years later that the splendid garden, that you see on your left as you approach the château, came into being. It is a square on which the gravel paths mark out a pattern like the crosses on a Union Jack, and the southern edge is the bank of the Cher.

In the same year, Philibert Delorme was commissioned to join the château to the southern bank by a bridge, completing a design which is believed to have been inherited from Katherine Briçonnet who, even with her husband's wealth, had never been able to make it a reality. But now the King had found a solution to the financial problem. A tax of twenty livres each was imposed on every public bell in the kingdom, and the proceeds were devoted to easing the pressing financial needs of Diana.

The parallel in the first book of Rabelais' *Gargantua* gave great joy. Gargantua was in Paris, listening to the bells: 'Which, whilst he was doing, it came into his mind, that they would serve very well . . . to hang about his mare's neck.' It was all very well for the ribald citizens of Paris to joke about the King's Mare, and the bells he had hung around her neck, but such irreverence was not welcome in Touraine. At Chenonceau, Diana was a popular and well-liked chatelaine.

The final touches were being made to the new bridge in June, 1559, when news came of the King's accident in a tournament. To Catherine it would have been a startling confirmation of the vision of Nostradamus, recorded many years before:

'The younger Lion will the elder vanquish
On Bellona's Field in a singular duel,
Within the Golden Cage his eyes will be put out,
Two wounds in one, and then to die a death most cruel.'

This, we must not forget, had already been printed in a book dedicated to the living monarch whose death was thus so accurately foreseen. After an indecisive tilt with the younger Montgomery, Henri insisted on a second run. The affair became a 'singular duel', with only the two participating after the end of a friendly set-to on the tournament ground. Montgomery's broken lance, sliding off the King's shield, penetrated the cage-like golden helmet, pierced neck and eye, 'two wounds in one'. The King's death was indeed most cruel, for he lingered, in atrocious pain, for eleven days.

From this moment onwards, Catherine's love was centred on the youngest of her three sons, as if she had read, only too clearly, the meaning of that other verse in that same book already quoted which told her that the young François would die before he was eighteen.

To Diana, Henri's death marked the end of a virtual reign as Queen and put her own life in peril.

Her feelings did not show upon her face, if we may believe Brantôme, the flattering (and scandal-mongering) commentator of the times: 'I saw her when she was seventy years of age, as beautiful of face, and as kind, as when she was thirty. Above all, she had a very white skin, without using paint or powder. But it was said that every morning she used some decoction and other drugs of which I know nothing.'

Catherine became widow, and Regent, on July 10. On January 4, of the following year her little revenge was complete; Chenonceau was exchanged for Chaumont. The third of the ladies of Chenonceau entered into possession.

Then the Chenonceau that we know came into being, and was even more magnificent than as we see it now. Catherine had no great wish to walk in the garden bearing her rival's name, and made her own on the other side of the château. It is an interesting sidelight on her character that her own garden is smaller than that of Diana; smaller, yet quite perfect. Catherine arranged for the making of a great park. Catherine ordered the building of that superb gallery on the new bridge that has given Chenonceau its present renown. Chenonceau, in fact, owes little to Diana and much to Catherine. What we cannot see today is the magnificent furniture, the lovely statues, the splendid ornaments and the countless books she had brought to Chenonceau from Italy.

The new young King made his solemn entry into Chenonceau, with his girl-wife, Mary Stuart, on the one side, and Catherine on the other. The full length of the avenue was lined by the peasants in their Sunday best, with rough banners flying, drums beating and the children shouting until they were hoarse. To receive them were 'Victory and Renown, dressed in the antique fashion,' making deep obeisance as the royal party approached, and from a balcony, Pallas herself threw down upon the King a rain of flowers.

That was on March 31. On December 5, the King was dead; the little Queen soon to quit France and to face her destiny as Mary, Queen of Scots.

It was three years later that another young King was welcomed at Chenonceau; the festivities were even more elaborate. As Charles IX approached, sirens emerged from the little canals bordering the drive, singing their songs of praise. Hardly had their last note sounded when nymphs emerged from the shadow of the trees echoing the theme, until sirens and nymphs alike disappeared shrieking into water and into woods as the satyrs, all clad in cloth of gold, with hair of silk, came running in to ravish them.

But virtue must ever triumph, and here, to great applause, come charging the gallant cavaliers, dressed 'in incarmined silver and velvet blue' to drive off the satyrs and rescue the fair nymphs and sirens. Then all advanced to pay homage to the King.

Four days the festivities went on, with cannonades from the terrace, with firework displays brought specially from Italy, with dances and masquerades, with mock naval combats on the Cher, and with the little island in mid-stream 'made into a terrestrial paradise with hidden music . . .'

The years passed; there came the eve of Saint Bartholomew to make a bloody counterpart to the gay festivities at Chenonceau. It was the defeat of the Protestants, the triumph of the Guises. It heralded the death of Charles; he died, dreaming day and night of the blood that ran.

The third son, the favourite, once King of Poland, came to the throne as Henri III. Chenonceau again was filled with the sound of revelry, the light of torches. This time the fête caused open scandal. Its cost was fantastic: 100,000 livres. The meals were served by ladies of the Court, 'half-naked, their hair falling upon their bare backs.' Festivity had become licence.

The worst was still to come.

Catherine had ordered the celebration; the King undertook to provide the entertainment. The tables were set up in Catherine's new garden. The King's *divertissement* was about to begin. Who was this approaching, this mincing girl, this overpainted, overdressed creature, this horrid parody of womanhood? The King. And these others with him, only a little less revolting? The Duc d'Anjou and the gentlemen of the King's Court. This time the Protestants were not alone to protest against the iniquities of a Court that threatened to call down upon France the fate of Sodom and Gomorrah; the pulpits of the Catholic Church thundered forth their protest.

Who can wonder that the Duc de Guise, the first gentle-man of France, the iron warrior, the perfect courtier all in one, felt himself greater than the King? A lesser man he could hardly be.

Dark days indeed now came to Chenonceau. From her favourite dwelling, Catherine wrote an indignant letter on receiving the news of her daughter-in-law's execution, the little Mary of whom she had always a kind word to say, and to save whose life she had herself pleaded to Queen Elizabeth: 'I am sick at heart to see the little respect the Queen of England has shown to the message you gave her on the King my son's behalf; she has shown a great disdain and full little care of the consequences . . .' However much she might have felt for Mary herself, the insult to 'the King my son' affected her most. Her Benjamin could still do no wrong.

She left for Blois, never to see Chenonceau again. Came the eve of Christmas, the unmanly King pulled down the great warrior. The troubled Catherine survived only a few days. Chenonceau and the debts appertaining to it passed to her other daughter-in-law, Louise de Lorraine, the fourth and most tragic of the ladies of Chenonceau.

None of these Renaissance ladies are very easy to under-stand; Louise de Lorraine is at once the simplest in character end the most baffling of them all.

Her husband had been King for fifteen years when, as qse was passing the heat of summer at Chenonceau, by the ɔool waters of the Cher, a messenger reached her to tell qer that a fanatical monk, Jacques Clément, had, the day qefore, stabbed and wounded His Majesty. There came too a letter from Henri: 'My darling (*ma mie*), I hope that I shall be quite all right; pray to God for me, and do not move from there . . .'

By the time this letter reached her, Henri III was dead, and France had no King.

Louise obeyed him to the letter. When she knew for certain of his death, she shut herself up in Chenonceau. She took the white mourning of royalty. Her own room and little oratory were hung with black, ornamented with silver tear-drops and *memento mori*, some of which may be seen in the Gallery. 'Pray to God for me, and do not move from there.' For ten long years she prayed for him by day and by night; for ten long years she never left Chenonceau. 'La Dame Blanche', they called her, The White Lady, whose whole life was spent in prayer, in needlework, and in reading. Her ghost, they say, can still be seen on a moonlit night watching from one of the windows, rosary in hand, murmuring those prayers for the soul of her husband of which he stood in such dire need.

It is incomprehensible. In all France, one would have said, there could be none to regret him, since his mother's death. How is it possible that a widow should mourn ten years for this weak and vicious and perverted specimen of humanity? She remembered only the man who, on his death-bed, thought of her enough to send a last kind and reassuring letter. Nothing else in his life became him so well.

She has left no mark upon Chenonceau, this gentle Louise de Lorraine: no garden of her own, no wing that is hers, no place that bears her name. All that is left is a white, shadowy figure that a handful of people imagine they have seen, no more than a trick of moonlight reflected in a window. A little white flicker lights for a moment on one of the pages of history, and is gone.

The people of Chenonceaux fell upon evil times; the château lay empty, falling into disrepair, the gardens became overgrown with tares, the untended park reverted to moorland. The sixteenth century gave place to the seventeenth, and the seventeenth to the eighteenth, before the sound of revelry was heard there again.

In 1733, the Duc de Bourbon sold Chenonceau to a
certain M. Dupin. The wheel had turned almost the full
circle. The new, the present Chenonceau, was built with
the money of one state financier, Bohier; it was saved
from complete dilapidation by the money of another state
financier, Dupin, *Fermier Général.* The parallel is almost
perfect; in each case it was the wife who loved and made
the château her own and in each case she survived the
husband and ended her days peacefully on her own property.

Madame Dupin was an intellectual young woman of
twenty-six when first she came to Chenonceau; most
unfairly, other women felt, she was beautiful as well.
The combination of intelligence, beauty and great wealth
brought back to Chenonceau all the activity it had known
two centuries before; everybody who was anybody in
France came at her invitation to spend a week, or a fort-
night or a month in the summer or the autumn at Chenonceau. But first, with great energy and unlimited money,
the château had to be restored and cleaned, the gardens
re-established, the wilderness made once more into a park.

Madame Dupin was already forty when Jean-Jacques
Rousseau from Geneva, as M. Dupin's secretary, saw her
for the first time. 'Madame Dupin was still . . . one of the
most beautiful women in Paris. She received me at her toil-
ette. Her arms were bare, her hair loose, her dressing-gown
ill-closed. I was quite new to this kind of thing. My head
could not stand it. I trembled, I forgot myself. . .'

The lady was feminine enough not to be entirely displeased that a man should still lose his head a little over her;
far from being disgraced, Jean-Jacques was kept in the
service of the family as tutor to the children. It was then
that he came to Chenonceau.

He was happy at Chenonceau, as he was never again to
be happy. He loved the children, and wrote his *Emile*
to help their education. In those celebrated *Confessions,*

he writes with affection of his time there. 'There was plenty of amusement in that beautiful place, and one ate extremely well there. I became fat as a monk.' Quite extraordinary is his claim to have written several pieces for three voices 'full of fairly strong harmony', for there is no other record of his having any ear for music, much less any gift for composition.

In the fulness of time, M. Dupin died. His widow, more and more in love with her beautiful country residence, spent ever more of her time there. In this quiet backwater the thunder of the coming Revolution was no more than a distant rumble.

The old Kings had chosen wisely when they built their castles in Touraine; the Revolution there was far less savage than elsewhere. That may be seen most readily from the fact that all the major châteaux were left intact, whereas in other parts of France a great number of them were sacked and burnt to the ground. There was, it appears, some talk of knocking down this odious symbol of the oppression of the poor, but nobody really believed in it. The people of Chenonceaux were well off when owners were in residence, and half-starved when it was left unoccupied. None who knew the kind and clever Madame Dupin could really wish her any harm, and no ill came to her or to her château. She died, peacefully, in the home she had made her own for some sixty-six years, in 1799, at the fine age of ninety-two.

The sixth of our ladies of Chenonceau does not make her appearance until a long time after the death of Madame Dupin. It was in 1864 that Madame Pelouze bought the château and restored it to the original Bohier design. She was one of the group of enlightened people of her time who deplored the fashionable taste for romantic 'Gothic' ruins. The new enthusiasm for the careful reconstruction of ancient buildings was largely the work of

Prosper Mérimée and Viollet-le-Duc, but it should be remembered in the favour of the much maligned Napoleon III and Empress Eugénie that little of this work could have been carried out without their interest and active support. Under Madame Pelouze, windows that Catherine de Médicis had opened up were closed again, and the caryatids between them were removed. Mercifully the restoration was exceedingly well done, and there is probably nothing in it to regret.

The château now belongs to the Menier family, to whom all who know and admire it owe a great debt of gratitude for the enormous sums they have spent in maintaining it in its present state of perfection. Katherine Bohier's four ground-floor rooms may be visited, together with the chapel, the library and the gallery. There is a great wealth of ancient furniture, Flemish tapestries of the sixteenth century and old pictures.

But for myself, the wonder of Chenonceau is not inside, but outside. Other buildings in which there has been much unhappiness in the course of centuries have, however faint, an aura of melancholy about them, but Chenonceau has none. It stands, serene and dignified, bright and almost gay, as if, invisibly blazoned upon it were the old sundial motto, *horas non numero nisi serenas*, remembering only the sunny hours, the laughter and the song.

It is, I think, the most beautiful domestic building, of any age, that I have ever seen, yet I should admire it the more if it conveyed also some impression of the dark empty days, the weeping and the anguish that complete its history.

CHAPTER IX

High Finance and High Politics
(MONTRICHARD AND VALENÇAY)

ALMOST any other château is an anticlimax after Chenonceau; it is best to face the fact, and relax.

The next one along the Cher is Montrichard; as a building, it will not stimulate you. The passing tourist, says the guide book, will content himself with taking in, from the old bridge over the Cher, the view over the ruined keep dominating the township and with seeing the ancient houses in the Rue Nationale. This is a little unkind to Montrichard, but one must agree that one old keep is very much like any other old keep. There is, nevertheless, one important omission. The old houses ought to be seen, particularly the 'Ave Maria' house with the Annunciation carved on the corner upright, but any visit should include also a few quiet minutes in the ancient Romanesque Church of the Holy Cross.

Louis XI had a daughter, Jeanne de France. Under Salic law she could not become Queen in her own right, and there was no male heir-direct. The King could not bear that the throne should not pass to his line, and looked round for a way out. It was not hard to find. His heir-apparent, the descendant of his grandfather's brother, was not within the forbidden degree of consanguinity. The wily Louis arranged a marriage.

Of all the cathedrals and churches of France in which so

important a ceremony might have been held, who would
have thought of this little church of the Holy Cross in a
remote village? Even from a strictly practical viewpoint it
was most unsuitable; how could the great crowd of princes
and nobles be housed in this small nave? Whether Louis
had qualms of conscience, or whether it was just fear of
public ridicule, the wedding was as quiet as if it had been
that of a country squire. There was no overcrowding of
the nave, for there were as few witnesses as possible, and
for excellent reasons.

The bridegroom was a pleasant-faced, upstanding boy
of fourteen years of age. The girl-bride, for all that she
was Jeanne de France, the first lady in the land, 'had a
double hunch on her back, congenital disease of the hip,
and a veritably simian appearance.'

In the cool and quiet of the little church one can meditate
on the disadvantages of being born a future King.

Towards Saint-Aignan are great quarries, from which
came much of the local freestone. The cliffs are pitted with
caves, some now used for growing those mushrooms that
help to make the local dishes so palatable, and some still
serve as troglodyte dwellings.

I have known Britons and Americans wax indignant that
in the present advanced state of civilisation human beings
should be condemned still to live in caves. To which
the tenants reply that the caves are warm and dry, draught-
free and noise-proof, which is more than can be said of
many modern houses. But the greatest possible argument in
favour of them is a very recent one; thanks to the extremely
advanced state of our civilisation they have become emin-
ently desirable dwellings, more so than ever before in the
long history of their occupation; they are nearer proof
against an atom-bomb attack than any man-made house.

Saint-Aignan itself is the almost perfect village. The
ground rises up from the left bank of the Cher and the little

houses rise on the side of this natural amphitheatre, beam-and-plaster houses of the fifteenth and sixteenth centuries some of them, standing at quite impossible angles. Above them is a tall church of the earliest Gothic style, and above the church is a Renaissance château, approached by a stone stairway far too magnificent for its purpose.

The whole village has an extraordinarily artificial appearance, and seen from far off it resembles nothing so much as the model village in the Christmas window display of one of the large Paris department stores. The church, though, is solid enough and real enough, in good sound stonework of the twelfth century, with mural paintings to remind us that in early days at least the House of God was a blaze of colour inside and not the cold and cheerless grey to which we are accustomed and which contrasts so strongly with the whole idea of Christian joy.

The road by the Cher comes to an end at Selles-sur-Cher, where the old abbey is now part town hall and part post office; the way now lies due south to Valençay.

Modern times catch up with us again at the little town itself; its centre was pillaged and then burnt by the Germans in 1944; many of the inhabitants were massacred. The château remains untouched.

Valençay château is unique; it is a monument of the decadence of Renaissance art. 'Sumptuous', the guide books call it. Impressive it certainly is, but impressive as only the alliance of great wealth to inborn bad taste could make it in an age of appreciation of beauty. Its period saves it.

Somewhere around the year 1540, Jacques d'Estampes knocked down the then existing feudal castle and began building a new residence for himself. He was full of the pride of his blue blood. He had recently married the daughter of a financier, and his wife's money went to his head. A d'Estampes deserved the finest château in the country;

this d'Estampes now possessed the means to express his pride in stone.

That was how Valençay began. Later owners added to it and modified it to suit their own tastes, and contributed to its oddity and to its heaviness. For instance, entrance is by an enormous square keep, but a keep bearing as much relation to a feudal fort as a poodle with a yew-tree clip has to a mastiff. It is a keep with an excess of windows, with ornamental turrets, with machicolations as false as the worst that Victorian Gothic ever gave us. The steep roof is broken by round dormers and surmounted by fantastic chimneys. Superimposed pilasters have Doric capitals on the ground floor, Ionic on the next, and Corinthian on the second, all helping to confirm the impression of a builder determined to incorporate a little of the best of every style, much as Ruskin recommended that every house should have something Gothic about it, were it only a single Gothic window.

At each end of this block, and of the block completing the building and standing at right angles to it, are fat, round towers of a girth utterly disproportionate to their height, grossly and offensively disproportionate. They might have been saved by the tall, conical roofs characteristic of the sixteenth century, instead of which they have cumbersome domes ending in lanterns and giving an impression of heaviness and a little reminiscent of old Moscow and entirely different from the grace and lightness of a Chenonceau, or indeed of many a less celebrated château.

The east wing was added in the seventeenth century and carries the Classical-Renaissance-Oriental style of the rest into further disparity by adding the fashion of Mansart, with alternating round and square dormers. The inner façade on the courtyard, refashioned in the eighteenth century, adds still another incongruity.

If Chenonceau disappoints in the least degree through

having an atmosphere too happy for its history, Valençay will not; it carries a centuries-old aura of ostentatious wealth. A whole succession of financiers possessed it for their brief moment, and went the way of all financiers. In 1719, His Excellency the Councillor of State and Comptroller General of the Finances of France, John Law of Lauriston, entered into an agreement to purchase it, at the height of his rocket career. Before he could take over, inflation caught up with him and he fled the country; the sale was cancelled in 1720.

Not for nearly another century does a really outstanding character come into its history. This time it was Charles Maurice Talleyrand de Périgord, Bishop under the Monarchy, Director of the *Département* of Paris under the Revolution, proscribed under Robespierre, Foreign Minister under the Directory, Minister again under the Consulate, Prince under the Empire, Foreign Minister at the Restoration, Prime Minister after the Hundred Days, Duke of Valençay on his retirement, Ambassador to the Court of Saint James under Louis-Philippe. 'Kings may come and Kings may go, but I go on for ever.'

Is there any parallel to such a career in any other country? He would be a rash novelist who would dare to invent such a character.

Talleyrand must start with our sympathy. His father was an officer in the Army of Louis XV during the Seven Years War. Charles, as a child, met with an accident which lamed him for life. His father, considering him unfit for the only occupation worthy of a Talleyrand, the Army, disinherited him. After a lengthy *procès*, the rights of primogeniture were transferred to a younger brother. Charles, who longed for the one career barred to him, found to his fury that he was destined for the Church.

He was, from all the evidence available, a complete unbeliever. He saw in the Church only a means of attaining his ambition, and his ambition grew and grew until nothing would satisfy him but to become the master of France. He was not greatly gifted academically, but by hard work made himself a fair scholar at school, seminary and Sorbonne. The latter made him, or rather he made himself whilst at the Sorbonne, a cynic and a rake. He acquired a reputation as an agreeable young wit.

His immorality was notorious. That in itself was no bar to promotion in the Church. In 1775, at the age of twenty-one, he became Abbé of Saint-Denis; at twenty-six he was Agent-General to the French clergy; at thirty-four, Louis XVI appointed him Bishop of Autun.

He was, in De Quincey's phrase, a 'rather middling Bishop, but very eminent knave.' Eminent he certainly was, for the clergy of his diocese appointed him to represent them at the calling of the States General. He was one of the members who drew up the Declaration of Rights. The future was confused, unpredictable; Talleyrand therefore made friends of all those who might rise to power, Sieyès, Lally-Tollendal, Mirabeau; whatever happened he would have a friend at Court. He put himself forward as an authority on the Constitution, on finance and (with considerable reason) on education.

All his life, Talleyrand kept one ear to the ground to detect the coming movement of the masses. He had now no doubt as to the general future trend of affairs in France, even if he could not yet determine which of his new friends would rise to direct them. The Church was going to be of little further use to him; he could afford to disregard it. In 1789 he went so far in his bid for popularity with the masses as to propose confiscation of all the Church's landed property; it brought him the desired result, the office of President of the Assembly. The Church, alarmed too late at the viper it had nursed, brought pressure to bear; cynically he took the oath to the Constitution in

15. VILLANDRY. '*Immediately below the keep is the highest of the terraced gardens, the exquisite* Jardin d'Amour.'

16. LANGEAIS. 'Interesting as being the last unspoiled castle of this period still left to us, complete with drawbridge and portcullis.'

1791 and at the same time consecrated two new bishops and declared his sincere attachment to the Church. The Church was not to be appeased any longer by his meaningless words; Talleyrand was excommunicated.

His first career over, he attacked his new one, unashamed, unshamable. He followed Mirabeau as Director of the *Département de la Seine* (Paris). Ear to the ground again, he showed that he could feel public opinion forming before any other man of his time. Before the Terror could turn the public away from their new leaders, Talleyrand got himself sent to London on an exceedingly unofficial mission to reconcile Pitt to the Republic. There seems little doubt that some of Mr. Pitt's gold found its way into his possession. In 1792, he was proscribed. He was quite unconcerned; he knew that the Revolutionary tide was about to turn.

As he had foreseen, he was recalled to France after the fall of Robespierre. With his usual disconcerting accuracy, he picked on Barras as the coming man, attached himself to him, and in due course became Foreign Minister under him, in 1797.

Needless to say, he foresaw the rise of Napoleon. He disliked him personally, and distrusted his judgment, but accepted him for the moment as France's man of destiny.

Then came a setback sufficient to sink any ordinary politician for ever. He was disgraced for having, against suitable remuneration, naturally, attempted to reconcile the British Government with the rebels in the American colonies. Small wonder that Mr. Pitt's gold is an ever-recurring theme in French memoirs and histories of the period. Every ill that beset France was attributed to it; the widespread belief in the perfidy of Albion, and the hidden power of the British Secret Service, which for over a hundred years poisoned Franco-British relations, dates mainly from Talleyrand's almost open acceptance of British bribes.

K

Talleyrand bounced back like a rubber ball. He won Napoleon's good graces again by taking an active part in the shocking murder of the Duc d'Enghien, the lowest depth to which he sank. It called forth Josephine's scathing 'cursed cripple', and that, in its turn, made her his enemy. It can probably never be known how much he contributed to her downfall. Talleyrand threw all his gifts into helping to make Napoleon, first, Consul for life, then Emperor.

It was at this point in his career that he became the owner of Valençay. Here, in this pretentious château so suitable to his tireless ambition, he weaved the plot that partially succeeded in breaking up Britain's coalition in 1805. He felt no more bound by Mr. Pitt's gold than by any sense of loyalty to any French master he served. Here, in these vast rooms, on these great terraces, he could receive and suitably impress those relatively humble people he found so useful. Here he sized them up; this man has a price in money, this one a price in honours, this third one needs no payment beyond further inflation of his native self-importance. He used men and women cynically and ruthlessly; he pounced on their weaknesses; he flattered their failings. Perhaps what we cannot forgive him is the number of times his cynical appreciation of human character proved to be right.

From 1805 to 1808 Valençay served him for this useful purpose. Then came the war in Spain. As irritatingly right as ever, Talleyrand opposed it. However, King Ferdinand was brought a prisoner to France. He was of no use to Napoleon, who could not conceive that a Buonaparte might not make a good King of Spain, or that the people might not wish to keep him. To the far-seeing Talleyrand, Ferdinand was a potentially valuable friend. The exiled King's prison was Valençay.

For six years Ferdinand lived at Valençay in considerable comfort and reasonable state. The park, which still measures some 5,000 acres, was then some 25,000 acres in extent. The King could ride and drive and hunt within the domain; the vast rooms were not unworthy even of a King of Spain; far more than these material advantages, the open friendship of Talleyrand must have helped to make his exile tolerable, for in the friendship of a time-serving politician of uncannily accurate foresight lay the virtual proof of the certainty of an eventual return to his fatherland and his kingship.

Talleyrand became a Prince of the Empire, Prince Bénévent, but his career under Napoleon was ended. Napoleon had already taken very badly his criticism of the Spanish war, now Talleyrand's outspoken condemnation of the Russian campaign brought final rupture. Once more he showed that magnificent sense of timing, and got out before he could be involved in, or blamed for, the coming catastrophe. The year was 1814.

More scheming and plotting as Talleyrand made himself the hated but inevitable link between the Allied governments and the Bourbons. His very name was anathema to both sides, yet he dominated the situation to the extent of dictating to the Senate the terms of Napoleon's surrender. Louis XVIII could do little else than accept him, and rely on him, as Foreign Minister. Wisely, too, for he made the voice of France effectively heard at the Congress of Vienna.

It is consoling to know that the Hundred Days caught him as completely by surprise as it did all the others. Louis XVIII fled to Ghent; Talleyrand forsook him callously and completely.

When the Hundred Days were over, the furious Louis refused to have anything to do with him; the Allies refused to deal with anyone else. Talleyrand was more powerful than the King, and returned as Prime Minister. Not for long, so intensely disliked and distrusted was he by all; not even a Talleyrand could endure that atmosphere, and his career was virtually over. As a thank-offering for being rid of him, Louis made him Duke of Valençay.

He still remained a power to be reckoned with. In his most innocent moments at Valençay, intrigue was only just around the corner. Much as he might like to pretend to be now no more than a simple country gentleman, power politics still possessed his mind. His hand, more than any other, made the July Revolution, and brought Louis-Philippe into power. Almost automatically, Talleyrand was offered the Ministry of Foreign Affairs.

The new Duke of Valençay had his doubts about the durability of the Louis-Philippe régime and preferred to end his official career as Ambassador, fully accredited this time, to the Court of Saint James. Valençay saw him no more; in 1829 he made it over to his nephew, Napoléon-Louis (a nice reminder of the uncle's many allegiances) Talleyrand, from whom the present owner is descended. He retired, a weary old man, in 1834, and died four years later.

The great park of Valençay is now a zoo; of all the strange animals in captivity there, not one is more difficult to understand, not one less self-sufficient, not one less human, than Prince Bénévent, Duke of Valençay. He was born, or he forced himself to become, incapable of the ordinary human virtues: love, generosity, charitableness, loyalty. One can even pity him for having spent his life unaware of the rich rewards of disinterested friendship. He defies the best efforts of the biographer, as a being too foreign to our understanding for us really to picture the working of his mind at all. Thomas Carlyle has an illuminating phrase about him: 'a man living in falsehood and on falsehood, yet not what you could call a false man.' That is true; whatever he did, he could claim to have done for the good of France.

What cannot be forgiven him is the example he set future

politicians. If only he had not been successful, later politicians who have thought that they too could save France
by betraying their fellows would not have followed in
his footsteps. Laval was the outstanding example. The man
was, in Talleyrand's way, a patriot. He was convinced he
could twist the occupying Germans round his little finger.
He believed that Russia and Britain would fight with Germany until all three were exhausted and France, with Laval
in power, would bestride the European scene, intact and
wealthy, and impose her own peace for the good of the
nations. As with Talleyrand, no action was too mean, no
betrayal too cruel, if it served this purpose.

Chance brought me up against another and a lesser one
during the battles for the liberation of France in 1944.
He had been a member of the 'Capitulation Cabinet' of
1940. He was a badly frightened man when he came into
our hands, yet he was pitiful, not because he was old and
frightened, but because he was a disciple of Talleyrand.
He still thought in terms of the powerful political friends
he had made in all parties, of France's coming need (in his
opinion) of men of his great political experience and knowledge. He could look forward to a time when France would
call on him again to serve in a Cabinet, perhaps even to
be Prime Minister. He was conscious of no betrayal, only
of having made a political mistake 'which the public will
soon forget'. He still lives, in disgrace and in a state of
great moral indignation at the injustice of the prison sentence he served. Laval is dead, assassinated. Let us pray that
the lesson, that to be a Talleyrand needs the genius of a
Talleyrand, has now been learned, and that there will be
no more disciples to win the hatred and contempt of their
fellow-beings during their lifetime, and to earn the execra-
tion of historians after their death.

As the limping ghost of Valençay is not a pleasant subject
on which to end a chapter, let us turn to one excellent

thing that comes from the little village. It is the Valençay goat's milk cheese, admirable accompaniment to a bottle of Bourgueil, a 'little' wine from another village in the Loire valley, half-way between Tours and Saumur.

It would be most improper to leave the Cher without a mention of the white wines produced on the slopes of its valley. They are difficult to find beyond these immediate places, because 'they don't travel'. In many cases, and with modern means of transport, this is just nonsense; in truth the answer is always the same, the vineyards are small, the output limited, and the people of the Loire have the good sense to keep it for themselves. Export the good wine of the Cher to earn the money to pay for wine of Algeria or the Languedoc? Really, only the British are mad enough in their post-war, export-conscious lunatic asylum to find any profit in that kind of transaction.

So these dryish white wines, with a flavour of their own impossible to describe (what idiotic words, incidentally, the experts use to describe the flavour of wines: 'flinty'; have you ever tasted a flint, or having done so, would you really appreciate a wine that had a flavour of it?) have to be taken on the spot; an excellent stuffed bream from the river is the dish to take with them. As the recipe for stuffed bream begins 'wash the fish in twelve different waters' I fear it is useless to continue with it for Anglo-Saxon readers.

CHAPTER X

The Black Years

(MONTRÉSOR AND LOCHES)

THE road eastwards from Valençay, towards the Loire again, runs along the edge of the Forest of Gâtine, the birth-place of fairies, the haunt of witches. In spite of myxamatosis, there are still rabbits here in considerable numbers. I have never seen any serious work devoted to the inter-connection between fairies and rabbits, but the link must be a strong one. On my own Sussex Downs, fairy rings invariably grow where rabbits are most numerous. In Brittany, a country notoriously pullulating with fairies, rabbits abound in all the places where they are to be found. A rabbit-warren doubtless provides an excellent retreat for the fairies to dive into when any human-being over the age of five approaches. As there is no possibility of my ever having any opportunity of investigating this phenomenon, I leave the thought to any who may care to enquire further.

Witches, it appears, even in this relatively remote part of the countryside, are by no means as plentiful as they used to be, and Walpurgis' Night passes off without any open scandal (how horrified that poor British saint would have been if she could have foreseen with what goings-on her name was to be associated). Nevertheless, curious-looking old women, living alone, are not unknown in the heart of the countryside and, notwithstanding cars and radios and all the noise and smell accompanying the benefits of civilisation, are still consulted on all sorts of things for which there is no very scientific explanation, such as why the butter refuses to solidify in the churn, and why the dog howls at night for no reason at all, and how to make the herbal decoction which clears the spots off the baby's face when the doctor's medicine couldn't. I can just remember, as a small boy, meeting one in Sussex; she had come down with the other old women to sack the potatoes on the farm. Her great beaked nose practically touched her chin, just leaving room between them for the stem of a dirty, stinking old clay pipe to stick out. I am not so sure now that the word 'witch' was applied to her strictly in the technical sense, but I do remember that she was reputed to have the best hand with warts in the whole of the south of England, at the very reasonable rate of one penny each, paid in advance.

Such bent old women are to be seen in the forests of Touraine and, in true fairy-story fashion, they are either gathering dry wood for the fire or searching about for some mysterious thing that grows. They are the last holders of the unwritten knowledge of the countryside, for they can hardly survive the Welfare State; it is time now to seek them out and to record their knowledge of herbs and simples, of weather-lore, of signs of plenty and of scarcity. Doubtless they believe much nonsense, but equally certain is it that in many respects science has not caught up with them yet.

The life of any one of them would not have been very safe in the high days of the first château reached along this road, Montrésor, for when the original builder, Foulques Nerra, Count of Anjou, was in one of his fits of repentance, the burning of a witch laid additional emphasis on his short-lived piety.

In this part of the world, Foulques Nerra is a useful

name to remember. You can acquire a reputation for learning quite easily thanks to him. Every time you come to
an old keep that looks as if it might, at least in foundations,
date back to the tenth century, you have but to look and say
'Ah! One recognises the work of Foulques Nerra', to be
right more times than not. Between here and Saumur he
built some twenty keeps, most of which either still stand
or have been, like this one, rebuilt.

Foulques was born in 972, becoming Count of Anjou
at the age of seventeen. He was exceedingly dark (and
known as 'Black Foulques'), short, thickset; he was reputed
the finest horseman of his age. The story is told that he rode
straight from Angers to Saumur, took part in a battle, and
rode back again without dismounting. The one part of the
story that is certainly true is the taking part in a battle.
He did little else all his life. Wherever there was a worth-
while battle in the offing, Foulques would be there. He did
not mind very much whose side he fought on so long as it
was a good fight, but being a shrewd gentleman he usually
derived some advantage from it.

He suffered, at intervals, from a very tender conscience.
After he had sacked two or three towns and villages and
put the inhabitants to the sword, he would build a church,
or a monastery, for the ease of his mind. The slaughter,
in a fit of temper, of one of his best friends sent him off
as a pilgrim to Jerusalem. As he approached his seventieth
year, which few men attained in those days, he decided
once and for all to put himself in the right. Off to the Holy
Places he went again, rope round his neck, with two servants
to scourge him at suitable intervals. In, we hope, a proper
frame of mind he set out on the return journey, but at his
age the scourging was too much for him, and he died of it
before he could reach Angers.

It would be idle to pretend that there is much of Black
Foulques' fortress left today, and what there is was heavily

restored a century ago, but it is at least an interesting example of its kind. The double surrounding walls are in part cut into the rock mass on which it is built; the rock itself is so full of cellars and caves that it is practically impossible to determine what is natural and what is artificial. The martial inner wall encloses a pretty garden in which stands a square manor house of the time of Louis XII, most delight-fully at contrast with it. It is so unexpected, with the self-conscious prettiness of its pinnacled dormers, that nothing about it can surprise one any more, not even the most interesting Polish pictures and souvenirs to be seen inside (it was sold to the Branicki family in 1849), a boudoir rich in Italian Primitives, and a superb solid mahogany staircase.

Beyond Montrésor the road crosses the plateau between the Indre and the Indrois; it is covered almost entirely by the 9,000 acres of the State forest of Loches, and you arrive suddenly at this little town across a bridge over so many different branches of the Indre that it is impossible to tell which is the river and which the backwaters amongst them all.

The view is dramatic; you come out of the timeless forest of noble trees full into the Middle Ages; the towers, the turrets, the roofs, the pinions, the little houses and the enormous castle of Loches so pressed in together, so utterly haphazard in their arrangement, so charmingly decrepit, that it is, for a moment, as unreal as a dream. Some of the streets of the town are inside the fortifications and some are out, and the whole place is so confusing that were it ten times bigger it would be no more difficult to lose your way. But what a joy it is to lose one's way! The most unexpected sights come into view round every corner; the turrets and carved window-surrounds of the Porte des Cordeliers, from the fifteenth century; the sixteenth-century Saint Anthony's Tower, which was the town's belfry from which the tocsin rang when danger approached; the enchanting

Renaissance Town Hall, which leans, almost literally, against the fifteenth-century town gate (Porte Picoys); the Chancellery, which still carries the royal symbols interlaced with the double 'D' of Diana of Poitiers.

Even if your wandering footsteps lead you to none of these, there are still the Renaissance houses themselves, the dwellings of the humbler people. Amongst them is that *Logis du Centaure*, where Hercules is carved alongside Nessus the Centaur, from which surely James Branch Cabell drew the first inspiration for *Jurgen*, whose adventures began in these parts. My generation read their *Jurgen* until they knew it almost by heart, but the much cleverer young men of today find his symbolism tediously simple, and forget the poetry and the pathos of this fairy-story of the fat-paunched, middle-aged pawnbroker whom (after a kind word for the Devil) Nessus carried away into the shadow-world with the body of a youth and the soul . . . of a fat-paunched, middle-aged pawnbroker. An admirable, if slightly improper, tale which colours still all this part of France for me.

The visit to the castle, or rather fortified camp, takes a long time and is exceedingly tiring. Comfortable footwear is an essential. The guide book states that 'the circulation of automobiles is possible, but the manœuvres are difficult', and that is a masterpiece of understatement. Any car that cannot be picked up and turned right round will involve you in such difficulties that you are likely to abandon it in despair after hours of horn-blowing, vociferous argument and contrary advice.

Entrance is through the portal of the château at the west side of the fortifications, in the middle of an irregular mass of masonry of the fifteenth century, flanked by two imposing towers of the thirteenth. Right at the beginning, in the portal itself, you will find yourself being inveigled into visiting museums. They are interesting enough as museums go; but refuse firmly to enter them if it is your first visit to Loches. Come back to them by all means, but if you visit them on your way to the château itself you will probably need a stretcher, or a new pair of feet, before you have finished.

To be fair, the *Musée du Terroir*, which occupies four large rooms in the portal itself, should be seen at some time. The country furniture and everyday objects of bygone years, as well as the costumes, of this part of the country are fascinating. Doubtless the geological collection will interest geologists. The other museum, the *Musée Lansyer*, has 400 landscapes from the brush of this local artist (rather a substantial morsel to swallow all at once), a reconstitution of his studio, and his art collections from China and Japan. Another room commemorates Louis Delaporte, another citizen of whom Loches is proud, who discovered the great temple of Angkor. Personally, I would prefer something about Agnès Sorel.

Having successfully resisted all attempts to persuade you into the museums, you find yourself, somewhat surprisingly, back into a street (*Rue Lansyer*) which leads to the peculiar one-time collegiate church, known as Notre Dame until 1806 and as Saint-Ours since then.

Saint-Ours started life as a Romanesque church in the twelfth century. It has an enormous porch, under which a piece of a Gallo-Roman pillar (according to some) or a Roman altar (according to the more romantic) serves as a recipient for the Holy Water. As you enter through the wide door and get your first view of the nave, you will find that another surprise awaits you. The absolutely unique vaulting is composed of two eight-sided stone pyramids. They are believed to be the work of Prior Thomas Pactius, who died in 1168; nothing of their kind had ever been done before, and nobody seems ever to have tried to repeat his experiment.

There is a great deal more about this church which is of considerable interest, including the curious mural painting in the crypt, but as this is a book about châteaux and not about churches I will add only that it is well worth the tip to the Sacristan to see the treasure, which includes Our Lady's girdle, to house which indeed the church was built. Whether or not you accept its authenticity (and there seems little reason to doubt that it came into being at the time of the Crusades, when the fabrication of such relics flourished), it is at least old enough to be exceedingly interesting.

Quite close to the church is the entrance to the *Logis du Roi*, the King's Palace itself. It is a mixed building; the north side (Charles VII) all turrets and crenellations; the south side (Louis XII) all decoration and dormers.

The happiest memories of Loches are those of a gentle creature, very much the sinner rather than the saint, the sweetest and loveliest of all the mistresses of the Kings of France, Agnès Sorel. Her tomb is on the ground floor of one of the towers of the *Logis*, an exquisite piece of work of the fifteenth century of which the creator is unknown. The seraphic expression on the face of the full-length statue of Agnès stretched out on her death-bed is one that you are likely to remember long after the flattering portraits of other royal favourites have long since passed from your mind.

The lovely oval of her face, the perfect bone formation showing through the covering flesh, would have made her a beautiful woman well into old age, had she lived. As it was, she died at twenty-eight, still in the fullness of her young womanhood. The face is unlined and still untroubled. It is a good face, in the sense that it reflects no evil in her life at all, a face impossible to associate with a hardened sinner.

In my ignorance I had always assumed that the artist had taken the usual liberties with his subject, that this was a face etherealised, intended to bear out her title, *Dame de Beauté*, Lady of Beauty. Then I came across a reproduction of Jean Fouquet's picture, *Virgin and Child*, of which the original, I believe, is in the *Musée Royal des Beaux Arts* in Antwerp. For long it haunted me and nagged at my memory. I knew I recognised it, had seen it before somewhere, yet I also knew that such could not be the case. It was a long time before I associated the two likenesses and found, of course, that I was far from being the first to do so. There is no doubt, no conceivable doubt, that the Antwerp *Virgin* is the Agnès of Loches. Jean Fouquet, the painter, was her devoted servant and friend in her lifetime, her executor after her death. There can be no mystery about whose face served as a model for the picture. There is, however, no record that I can trace of Fouquet ever having been a sculptor; he is known only as a painter, one of the creators of the art of painting in France. Such was his reputation that it is almost impossible that he could have been a sculptor as well, without leaving any record of this other side of his work.

We must assume therefore that the statue of Agnès on the tomb is the work of another artist entirely. If this be so, it is one of the few cases in which portraits of a royal mistress by two different artists, and in two very different media, give us an identical appearance. Agnès must have had the beauty they both portray, for if either or both of them had idealised the original (as was customary), it is incredible that the resultant idealised portraits from two different hands should be so exactly similar. Agnès, undoubtedly, was by far the most beautiful of all the mistresses of the kings of France.

It is somewhat of a shock to find a woman living in open sin serving as a model for the Virgin, though it is probable that the case is far from unique, for not all artists' models lived the purest of lives. Agnès, at least, was a repentant

sinner. This little country girl (she was born hereabouts
in 1422 in one of the smaller châteaux, daughter of a minor
noble) could not marry Charles VII. She became his mistress,
and that was almost her only fault. Her beauty drew all
manner of men to her. The King was a plain and worthless
creature. Yet she was entirely and utterly faithful and
devoted to him, and bore him children. She counselled him
wisely, restrained his excesses, made him appear a far wiser
man than he was, although, as might be expected from a
country-bred girl of little previous experience of the great
world, she had no idea of the value of money and was
hopelessly extravagant. Money could buy so many things
she wanted; the beautiful things she wanted in life for
herself; and for others, constantly in her thoughts, a happy
issue to their present difficulties. Her generosity was
legendary; above all, she spent bountifully on and for the
Church.

Supremely conscious of her own sin, she showered bene-
factions on the Chapter of the old church by the castle,
so that she might be assured of resting after death in a place
she loved and where she had been happy. For at Loches
she had been as happy as she had been unhappy at Chinon
where lived the Dauphin. The future Louis XI, the meanest
King that France would ever know, detested her, and the
chronicles give one to understand that he went as far at
times as slapping her face. At Loches she found content-
ment, but she knew how the Church disapproved of her
and would look on her as being unfit to be interred in
royal ground. So she bribed her way, as she hoped, into
lying after death where she wished to be.

It nearly failed. The clergy waited until Charles VII was
dead before remembering their scruples. So notorious a
sinner, they told Louis XI (doubtless expecting thereby
to please him), could not decently stay buried in their
church. Could they have her exhumed and the remains sent

up to the château for him to dispose of as he wished?

As they fully expected, the foxy King was quite agreeable to do a disservice to one dead with whom he had quarrelled so violently when living. But Louis XI was a man who put money above any personal feeling. Seeing, he reminded them, that she had paid them handsomely in her lifetime for the privilege of being buried in the church, it would only be right therefore that if they failed to keep their bargain, they should return the payment. Would they therefore kindly send back the gold with the remains? This counter-move brought consternation to the clergy; their scruples melted away; the King did not get Agnès' donations, and she stayed buried in the church until the Revolution.

That is not quite the truth, for she died at the great abbey of Jumièges in Normandy, and there her heart was kept. The other remains were transferred to Loches, where the unknown sculptor made her a worthy tomb. Then, during the Revolution, the soldiers of the battalion of the Indre, ironically, supposed it to be the tomb of a saint and broke it up. It was reconstituted in Paris in 1808 and transferred to this round tower of the *Logis du Roi* in 1809 where, thanks to a most beautiful piece of restoration we can admire it today.

The inscription tells how she came by the title of *Dame de Beauté*. It was a pun; Beauté was a property Charles VII gave her at Nogent-sur-Marne, near Paris, as properly fitting her beauty. Another little pun, in stone this time, is on the tomb itself: two lambs (*agneaux*) lie at the feet of Agnès.

Two angels bear her head. Of the three faces, hers is the most angelic. It is not perhaps so unfitting as at first it seems; in all her life she did no voluntary harm to anyone, she made no enemy but Louis XI (and that in itself was almost a virtue). When she died 'there was no gaiety and no beauty left in the realm'.

The *Logis* is really two buildings. One, the higher, is the *Vieux Logis*, pure fourteenth century; the adjoining one was added under Charles VIII and Louis XII and contains the attractive private chapel of Anne of Brittany, a mass of the most delicate carving.

Grim, depressing and fascinating are the towers. The tall white keep, overhanging a precipice, is the work of the twelfth century, as can be seen from the perfectly even masonry and the buttresses in the form of circular pillars. The lesser towers around it are from the thirteenth century.

Louis XI made Loches his state prison; here were performed all those acts of cruelty that made his name hated throughout France. In these towers he built the dungeons-below-the-dungeons which, in one of these towers, reach four floors down.

The Governor of this stronghold, and the Chief Gaoler, was the Prime Minister, Olivier le Daim. He was also the King's barber, and probably the only man that wretched monarch ever trusted.

Two of these *cachots* in the round tower contained the wood and iron cages supposed to be the invention of Cardinal Balue, Louis' Minister. In time, he himself sold his master's secrets to the Duke of Burgundy and was, it is said, imprisoned in one of his own inventions for eight years. The particularity of these cages was that they allowed the prisoner neither to stand upright nor to stretch out at full length. Personally, I have always had the greatest doubt about any man living in one for eight years; that he may have been put in it at intervals, as an additional punishment during the eight years, is conceivable, but could any human frame support a continuous period of such a length thus cramped? As for the story that Louis XI deliberately overfed him so that he grew too fat ever to be taken out, I think this is one of the less pleasant inventions of history.

L

Even Cardinal Balue did not hold the presumed duration-record for life in a cage. Duke Ludovico Sforza of Milan, *il Moro*, was imprisoned at Loches from 1500 to 1510, and supposedly in a cage. This twister and traitor, finally released, died of joy immediately on emerging into the light and air.

The number of prisoners was considerable in these vaulted dungeons, so ill-lit with their tiny windows. Their *graffiti* are still to be seen, though difficult now to read. To Philippe de Commines, the historian, is ascribed *Dixisse me aliquando penituit, tacuisse nunquam* (I have sometimes repented of having spoken, never of having kept silent). Distinguished men were some of the prisoners: The Duke d'Alençon, a Valois and possible rival; Charles de Melun (beheaded there in 1468 as a conspirator), and the Comte de Saint Vallier, father of Diana of Poitiers and opponent of the King's whims.

This miserable set of memories makes these stark towers, *donjon*, *tour ronde*, and *martelet*, almost alarmingly depressing; it is rather a relief to leave them and take the walk round the fortifications. At the foot of the keep a boulevard now occupies the site of the old moat. The south wall of the fortress is tremendous, dating from the time that Henry II of England fortified the town which he had inherited as Count of Anjou. He held it firmly enough; but whilst his successor, Richard Coeur-de-Lion, was prisoner in Austria, Philippe-Auguste intrigued with Richard's brother and rival, John Lackland, and got possession of it.

No sooner was Richard free than he rushed to recover it, attacking it with such fire that he took it by assault in three hours. Look up at the vast height and strength of this great fort, remember that where you stand on dry ground was a deep moat, imagine the arrows and the stones and the fiery pitch being hurled down from above, and you will wonder indeed how it could be done. To scale it with the means available at the time was no small feat even if it had been completely undefended.

The English held it for ten years, then Philippe-Auguste besieged it again (1205). This time, thanks partly to additional fortifications, it was a full year before it fell. Thereafter it remained a Crown fortress, and a prison.

This south front, still further strengthened during the thirteenth century, has three magnificent towers to interest the student of mediæval fortresses; they are not circular, but half-moon, the forerunners, and the first partial examples, of the bastion-flanking towers of the wars of siege.

Only this walk round gives a proper idea of the extent and the strength of Loches, but its great advantage is to lead you back into the heart of the little town, picturesque, human, warm and all the more enchanting after the memories of death and torture and hopelessness of the fortress itself.

In this contrast, Loches is quite unique, carrying you in a few hundred yards from the quaint and the pleasant to the cold and the harsh and the cruel, like life itself.

CHAPTER XI

Back to Beauty

(AZAY-LE-RIDEAU, VILLANDRY)

THE road from Loches alongside the Indre is one of the loveliest in this part of the country, curving away along the wooded valley and passing through small villages on the water's edge, each with a tiny *plage* or bathing beach, and canoes for hire, as well as the inevitable fishing boat. It is a timeless country in which life does not rush by but passes imperceptibly; the dozen old manor houses and little châteaux above the river, however old, have seen virtually no change below them through the centuries except for the actual traffic on the road. Beyond Courçay, whose main tourist attraction is a fountain that petrifies small objects dropped into its waters (which also operates with no haste at all), lies Montbazon, with another of Foulques Nerra's keeps; by this time the traveller should be penetrated by the peacefulness of his surroundings and be prepared to give the full measure of his admiration to Azay-le-Rideau, half-hidden amongst a curtain of trees, and surrounded by branches of the river.

For the moment he might well believe himself back again at Chenonceau, though the surroundings are not so impressive and, in spite of a strong family likeness, there is less grace in the building itself.

Azay was not always as peaceful as it now looks. In mediæval days a fortress covered the river, across which now runs the main road from Tours to Chinon. Eleven years before Charles VII was crowned at Rheims, when he was still a lad of fifteen and Dauphin, he passed by here. At that time the fortress was held by a Burgundian garrison. Charles' retainers and the Burgundians quarrelled. High words followed, some of them insulting enough to Charles himself. Flaming with anger, he called for an assault. His 500 men drove the Burgundians before them, took, sacked and burned the castle. The Burgundian captain and his 350 soldiers were all executed. For the next hundred years the village was known as Azay-le-Brûlé, Azay-the-Burnt.

In 1518, exactly one hundred years later, the property passed into the possession of Gilles Berthelot, married to a de Semblançay cousin, Philippa Lesbahy. Money marries money; Gilles Berthelot was Treasurer-General of the Finances of France and Mayor of Tours, and another member of the great clan of financiers who intermarried and formed one huge and powerful family. One way and another he was related to Katherine Briçonnet who built Chenonceau, to the Beaune-Semblançays, the Ruzés and the Fumées, in fact to all the wealth of the century.

Exactly as Chenonceau was built on the piers of the water-mill, so, a few years earlier, Azay was built on piles driven into the river bed. As Chenonceau was largely due to the will-power of a woman, so was Azay. Gilles had little enough leisure away from his task of collecting money for the King and for himself; the active supervision of the building of his new home was undertaken by his wife.

Related as we have seen, like Bohier, to the de Semblançay clan, Gilles took fright when the aged head of the house was brought to the scaffold, and fled the country. As with Bohier, an examination of his books 'proved' his guilt, and François I escheated the property. And again, as with Chenonceau, François did not know what to do with it once he had laid hands on it.

There the quite extraordinary parallel between the two châteaux ceases. Azay may be said to have had no further history, unless we except the entertaining episode of Prince Frederick Charles of Prussia in 1870.

The château had been occupied by the Prussian troops as a place sufficiently imposing to be a fit residence for the Prince, who began to live there in Germanic state. A tremendous Staff dinner was in progress, medals and epaulettes flashing beneath the light of an immense chandelier, when it suddenly came crashing down on their heads. It frightened them not a little, and the local inhabitants soon discovered that a frightened man is a very dangerous one. Prince Frederick Charles went about breathing fire and slaughter, swearing that a determined attempt had been made upon his life, and threatening to annihilate the village, the château and all the local inhabitants. The threat was all too likely to be carried out, and the inhabitants passed through a most uncomfortable time until the Prince was finally persuaded that the cause was purely accidental. The argument against the execution of his threat that seems to have had the most weight with him, was that to revenge himself upon the inhabitants because of a fallen chandelier might make him look ridiculous. So, less from humanitarian reasons than from pride, people, village and château were spared the Teutonic fury.

Knowing something of what went on in France during the last war, and believing that the national character changes very slowly indeed, I am of the opinion that the Prince was perfectly right when he assumed that the chandelier fell because it was intended for it to fall. On the other hand, it would have been an attempt on his dignity, not his life; killing your enemies by dropping chandeliers on them is a somewhat uncertain way of getting rid of them, and the bullet offered, in 1870, no less than during the last war, an easier and far more reliable means.

In other ways Azay differs considerably from Chenon-ceau. For example, it had an architect, Bastien François, where the latter did not. Then it was all built and finished in a single stretch of years, and a short one for the times and the magnitude of the work (1518-1529); no additions beyond outbuildings have since been made.

In its design it incorporates the features of the fortified castle of the Middle Ages, attenuated into the purely decora-tive. To them it adds the wealth of new decoration coming into fashion, and the total effect is only a little inferior to Chenonceau. In fact they are two sisters, with Azay (a little the elder) only failing to win the prize for beauty because the younger Chenonceau is even more lovely.

Coming from the village, the château is reached by a bridge leading to the 'court of honour', bounded on the farther side by one of the two main wings incorporating in its façade the front of its Renaissance staircase with tall, twin, wide-arched windows on each of the three floors. The other main wing is at right angles to the first, and ends in a completely round tower of considerable girth. The other angles of the building are rounded off by four smaller, protruding towers; all five have corbelled sentry-walks, purely decorative, and are surmounted by tall, conical roofs. The characteristic very steep roof over the rectangular wings are broken by huge, ornamented dormers springing from the line of the sentry-walk.

Over the chief portal is the salamander of François I (a compliment that Berthelot probably later regretted having paid), and the 'GB' of the proud owner. These devices are surrounded by complicated sculptures of unknown author-ship, which some consider worthy of Jean Goujon himself.

The influence of the then recent work at Blois is clearly to be seen in a similar use of pilasters, but the development of the newly-imported architectural ideas is to be found in the staircase. At Blois it stands out from the building and still turns round a central pillar; at Azay its façade is an integral part of the main frontage and rises straight inside from landing to landing. In design and ornamentation it is both elegant and elaborate. It has been considerably restored, and the parallel flights have been decorated with medallions of the Kings of France from Louis XI to Henri IV; only those of the second floor are genuinely of the time, but all are interesting and decorative.

In other respects, the interior has been little changed; the Beaux Arts have made it into a Renaissance Museum. This is very right and proper for, almost without exception, the furniture, tapestries, ornaments and pictures on show belong to the period of the château and might well have been there at the time it was inhabited by its original owners. The portraits (Emperor Charles V and his family, Catherine de Médicis, Cardinal de Guise, Duchesse de Guise, and Charles' sister, Mary of Austria) are fitting and interesting.

One entrancing part that the visitor is able to see is undoubtedly the kitchen, hung with ancient utensils; it needs but the wood fires and the crowd of cooks, the heat, the smoke and the smell, to live again instantly after four centuries.

It is impossible to walk all round the château, for on two of its sides it gives on the waters of the Indre. But from whatever angle you see it, whether from the courtyard or from the further banks of the streams, its lightness of design and whiteness of stone will fill your heart with delight.

Inevitably you will find yourself comparing it with Chenonceau, and I should be surprised if the same thought did not come to you as came to me. Seeing the relationship between the Berthelot and the Bohier families, is it not reasonably certain that Katherine Bohier came to visit here whilst it was building, saw it and admired it, and was urged to build an improved version on the even lovelier site of Chenonceau? To me it is quite impossible that there should be none but a chance connection between these two superbly feminine examples of Renaissance architecture. If I were a novelist I think I would like to embroider on a possible, but quite imaginary, jealousy between the two wives of financiers that led to the infinite pleasure of later generations of whom they never even thought in their rivalry.

Very different indeed are the aesthetic pleasures of Villandry, as masculine as Azay and Chenonceau are feminine. The original castle was of the twelfth century, or even earlier, for under the name of Coulombières, or Colombiers (the spelling of French place and proper names in the early days was as eccentric and individual as in England) it is known as the place at which Richard Coeur-de-Lion and Philippe-Auguste signed a peace treaty in 1189, and a lot of good it did them both. They were quite incapable of not fighting each other.

On the ruins and remains of the old fortress, Jean le Breton, who was Secretary of State to François I, built a fine Renaissance château somewhere about 1532, leaving intact as an integral part of the architectural scheme the fourteenth-century, castellated square keep which gives such strength to the conception. Part of the south frontage dates also from this time and is happily incorporated in the newer construction.

During the eighteenth century, when the Marquis de Castellane was its owner, it was completely transformed. Affected by the Anglomania of the time, the Marquis decided to sweep away the Renaissance gardens and to substitute for them a park in the English style. At the same time, presumably feeling that the Renaissance house looked out of place in these surroundings, he did his best to 'classicise' the building. The three frontages enclosing the 'courtyard of honour' lost their porticoed galleries on the ground level; and the dormers, their pinnacles; and the windows, their cross-bracing. The moats were filled in. The result was a hybrid without dignity or measure.

In the nineteenth century it passed into the ownership of Dr. Carvallo. Happy France, to find men willing to spend their private fortunes on its heritage of fine buildings. After considerable search, Dr. Carvallo found authentic drawings of the château as it had been before the alterations. With enormous patience, and at enormous expense, he rebuilt it with loving care exactly as it had been.

The surrounding eighteenth-century terrace has been swept away, and once again the château stands reflected in the waters of the moat. The arcaded galleries, cool always in the heat of a summer day, have been fully restored; the ornamented dormers once again relieve the monotony of the high roof.

Dr. Carvallo did more than restore the château; he filled it with lovely things. A great admirer of paintings of the Spanish school, he installed a museum of some interest, though I for one would have preferred pictures and objects of the Renaissance to those of Velázquez, El Greco, Morales, Ribera, Zurbarán and Goya which the visitor may admire there now, excellent as they are in themselves. There are, however, some delightful articles of furniture of the fifteenth and sixteenth centuries, very much in keeping with the château. This cannot be said for the Hispano-Moorish ceiling in wood, polychrome and gilt; it is a lovely thing and a splendid specimen of its kind, but so utterly alien in these surroundings, so entirely unexpected, that it produces a feeling of astonishment rather than admiration.

It is not, however, for what is inside, but for what is outside the château that visitors now come from all over the world. The work of Dr. Carvallo on the structure of the château has been carried on by his son, with the same integrity, in the gardens. They now represent the finest, almost the only, Renaissance gardens to be seen anywhere. He has in this but continued the work of his father, to whom we owe the rediscovery of the whole conception of the three-dimensional, architectural garden; but he has brought to it the results of patient research that have carried the reconstruction even beyond the point that would have satisfied his father. In its scrupulous accuracy it is staggering; in the perfection of its tending it equals anything that any King of France can ever have known, even though the King could draw upon an unlimited labour supply.

M. François Carvallo and his father have based their creation on all that is known of the work of the fifteenth-century gardener, du Cerceau (the best illustrations of his work are to be found, curiously enough, in the British Museum). They could not be certain, as they could of the stone-work, that the gardens are exactly as they were at Coulombières four centuries ago; they are certain, however, that these are true du Cerceau gardens, and that nothing grows in them that he did not employ in his own.

The twelve acres make a complicated lay-out, which it is difficult to visualise except from the air. The best place to see them is, in fact, from the top of the keep. Villandry is reached from Azay-le-Rideau by a secondary road heading generally north-west; we have therefore left the valley of the Indre behind us and are approaching the junction of the Cher and the Loire, towards which the distant landscape inclines. Immediately below the keep (which is on the south-west corner) is the highest of the terraced gardens, the exquisite *Jardin d'Amour*. It is separated from the château by a double file of orange trees in oaken tubs, standing like so many sentries. The shapes of the beds are determined by miniature hedges of box, clipped some twenty inches high, terminating in yew finials so perfectly formed that they seem quite artificial. *L'Amour Tendre* is there, hearts and flames shaped in box, and filled with two different reds; then comes *L'Amour Tragique*, swords (or are the smaller ones daggers?) of deeper, more tragic, reds. *L'Amour Volage* is more difficult to follow, but folded love-letters and butterflies (or moths) are there, in yellow and white and different reds. *L'Amour Fou* is a crazy carnival of twelve multi-coloured hearts all at sixes and sevens in a pattern which has neither beginning nor end.

In this topmost section is the one anachronism. I have mentioned at Blois the one-time existence of a *noria*, round which the blindfold ox would trudge his way hour after hour bringing up water in little wooden buckets on an endless chain, which spilled into the conduits and irrigated the whole gardens as well as supplied the fountains. M. Carvallo has not (or should I say, not yet) introduced this, and in order to provide for a water supply has made a decorative pool that is nearer the eighteenth or nineteenth than the sixteenth century in its appearance. The water is carried through the gardens by a canal; it is on the further side of this, and at the next lower level, that the kitchen garden comes.

The Renaissance conception of this is hard to explain in English when it is given so unpleasant a name as kitchen garden. Even to the most responsive, the decorative effect of the *jardin potager* must be difficult to appreciate when expressed in words. The patterned vegetables (no potatoes, of course) which include peas, and beans, and lettuce, and artichokes, and spinach, and onions, are most extraordinarily varied and beautiful; the secret of maintaining their staggering regularity I have not yet penetrated. Most will share my feelings that when we forgot how to make a vegetable patch a thing of beauty, we lost one of the most valuable artistic lessons of the Renaissance.

Even in the vegetable garden the architectural motive is not forgotten; it is decorated with rose-covered arbours and surrounded by a trellis on which grow the most beautifully trained cordon pears and apples.

The herb garden is not inferior to the vegetable garden; in one way it is its superior, for on a hot day the aromatic smell rises strongly, and the imagination is carried away to the spice-laden air of the distant East.

The maze I had always thought of as essentially English, to find that once again I was wrong. It was just another importation into England from a more civilised France, though I still think that we have the more perfect examples. Here the maze is of hornbeam, and will disappoint only those who remember Hampton Court when the maze there was better and more tidily kept than it is today, with its ice-cream papers and empty cigarette packets laying around. We may be thankful that no litter of this kind exists at Villandry; indeed such tidiness as we see in these gardens is almost inhuman.

No weed later than the sixteenth century, I am sure, would dare to poke its head through the ground here. Nevertheless, weeds of sufficiently ancient lineage to qualify abound, and the gardeners have never stopped in the relentless war against them. To see a horrified gardener spot one that has escaped his previous attention and pounce upon it as an eagle upon its prey, is not the least entertaining item in the day's visit to Villandry.

Little fountains, of course, are an essential of the architectural scheme, and are dotted everywhere, in every conceivable shape, and it goes without saying that the bigger waters carry dignified swans, more perfectly in keeping here in their surroundings than I have seen them anywhere else.

The greatest wonder of Villandry, to my mind, is the state of the sanded paths. These, instead of being the weed-ridden, untidy objects with which most of us are only too familiar at home, are part and parcel of the scheme of decoration. The sand lies on them thick. Gardeners trail rakes behind them, and leave a perfect pattern, and no footprints. Their eyes are unerring; it is an education to watch them circle the sometimes complicated outlines of the little fountains at the path junctions and, with real artistry contrive around them a sand-wave shape repeating the *motif* of the fountain base in diminishing ripples, until this sand-pattern melts into that of the paths themselves. One treads regretfully upon these paths, feeling a vandal to leave inelegant traces of sole and heel upon a minor artistic masterpiece.

All this work, I believe, is done by no more than five gardeners who must work far harder than any I know, and work with love. In all the gardens not a leaf, not a twig, is out of place; even the wind seems to respect them and not to blow them about.

M. Carvallo now has a world-wide circle of friends and admirers who come to him for advice, sometimes for seed, and often for the sheer pleasure of meeting a man who knows more about his own subject than any other living. Let us hope that the knowledge that he has so laboriously acquired has been recorded for future generations and will never again be lost, for Villandry is now that satisfying thing, perfection of its kind. The art of making it so should never be forgotten.

CHAPTER XII

Dark Ages and Fairyland
(LANGEAIS, USSÉ, CHINON)

AFTER Azay and Villandry, Langeais seems cold. It is
but a stone's throw in distance from Villandry, and
further away from it, in everything but geography,
than is easy to explain.

In the grounds are the remains of the old keep with
which (dare I write it?) Foulques Nerra in the year 990
began his career as a builder of fortresses; it has claims
therefore to be the oldest in France.

The 'new' château was begun some time in the thirteenth
century by Pierre de Brosse, who opened his career by
becoming barber to Louis IX, which was a quick way to
promotion. Obviously, the man who held the razor to the
King's throat in those troublesome times was in a position
of great esteem. The King could have a taster to ensure that,
if his food were poisoned, it would not be likely to reach
him, but nobody could defend him against the man, armed
with a dangerous offensive weapon, who was allowed not
only to approach the Royal Person but to lay his knife against
the Royal Throat. Pierre de Brosse was therefore a man of
trust.

Unhappily he did not stay a man of trust. Saint Louis'
son, Philip the Bold, who succeeded his father, inherited
Pierre de Brosse, and made him Minister. Philip's son died,
and was believed to have died of poison. Pierre de Brosse

accused the mother of this awful crime. In turn the mother accused the Minister, who was found guilty, and ended his days on the gallows at Montfaucon. The whole story presents one of the greatest mysteries in French history, and would make an admirable study if the records were only a little more complete. Did the boy die of poisoning at all? Much that the doctors of those days could not find an explanation for was put down to poison that now we would know to be a natural death, by peritonitis for example. If the boy was poisoned, was the mother guilty? If she were not, it was the most extraordinary thing for Pierre de Brosse to accuse her. The chance of his word carrying the day against hers was remote. If he were not telling the truth, why did he not find a lie that, even if not more plausible, would be at least more likely to find a better hearing? Did the trusted servant of two generations of Kings at last fall from grace? It seems quite possible that the boy died from natural causes, and that Queen and Minister accused each other in self-protection.

From this unhappy beginning sprang the château we see today. It was built on the foundations of de Brosse's 'new' château by another Minister, Jean Bourré, during the reign of Louis XI, between 1465 and 1469.

It is, then, as you might expect, more fortress than dwelling house. It rises at the foot of the little hill on which Foulques Nerra had built his keep; it has two wings at right angles, open towards the hill. The outer wall is stern, pierced by few windows, surmounted on this side of the castle by an unbroken sentry-walk nearly 450 feet round, and protected by three massive, conical-roofed towers.

Its grim appearance is due largely to the use of a dull grey stone; for the proportions are excellent and there is an unexpectedly domestic touch given by the many tall chimneys. It is interesting as being the last unspoiled castle of this period still left to us, complete with drawbridge and

17. LANGEAIS. *'Step around to the open courtyard at the back . . . and there is the forerunner of the Renaissance château. You have stepped suddenly and unexpectedly from war to peace.'*

18. USSE. *'The round white towers, holding more than reflecting the sunshine, for all their solidity are insubstantial as a dream.'*

portcullis. All the others have been transformed into something more gracious in intent.

Louis XI undoubtedly had it built to cover the road from Brittany, and placed it in the hands of a servant trusted as far as the old fox trusted any man. Incursions from the Celtic lands were still not infrequent, and sometimes obliged the King of France to wage a war on two fronts at once.

Langeais is astride two epochs; the warring Middle Ages, the coming Renaissance. The front is all warlike; but step round to the open courtyard at the back, the one that faces Foulques' hill, and there is the forerunner of the Rennaissance château. There is no sentry-walk here; the roof is ornamented with tall pointed dormers in the Gothic spirit; there are four or five times the number of windows. You have stepped suddenly and unexpectedly from war to peace, from the fifteenth century into the sixteenth.

It is a temptation to consider that the chief event for which the château is famous, the wedding of Charles to Anne of Brittany, was responsible for this, but actually this occurred twenty-two years after the completion of the building. The pinchbeck days of Louis XI were eight years finished; a new, and more luxurious spirit, had swept into the Court with Charles VIII of happier memory.

No more would the Breton gentlemen (a term which, owing to the smallness of the estates in Brittany, included most of the men in that province) come invading France or the defending fortresses be needed on either side of the frontier. A Princess of Brittany was now to be Queen of France.

The Queen's costume for the wedding at Langeais was 'a robe of cloth of gold, all covered in designs embossed upon it, gold upon gold'. Even the Court chronicler did not dare to call her beautiful; he covers his lapse with magnificent tact. The Queen, he writes, appeared 'the most noble and puissant of Ladies, as much in virtue as in

M

properties and seignories.' Plain she might be, but France never had a better or more sensible Queen.

Thanks to M. Jacques Siegfried, another of those public-spirited Frenchmen who have devoted their fortunes to the châteaux they have acquired, Langeais was admirably furnished, and internally restored, before his death in 1904. Everything is right about the furnishings of Langeais, which are as unique in their way as are the gardens of Villandry.

Forget the exterior, if you are tired by now of so many châteaux, and spend your time inside. Here, in the great room in which they were married, are Charles and Anne painted on wood; here in the dining hall, once the Guard room, is a huge fireplace that is a masterpiece of carving, due, it is claimed, to François d'Orléans; scattered through-out are tapestries, coffers, presses, sideboards, all of the fifteenth century, all pieces that might well have ornamented it in its great days. Here you will appreciate, as you can nowhere else, how the great men and women of the times loved beautiful things and tolerated the grim stone wall only on the outside of their castles. Inside, the tapestries that are now dim in colour were gay upon the walls; every piece of furniture, however utilitarian, was carved by artists to draw the eye away from the stone-work on to the warmth and polish of the wood; the very centre of attention, the fireplace, was a mass of ingenious carving, and on a cold night they could stand or sit around it and be amused by the complicated designs that, under the flickering light of torches, must have seemed to move and to have a life denied them by daylight and our modern forms of artificial lighting. The very beds were endued with a Gothic dignity and splendour that takes one's breath away. Into such an architectural contrivance, wide enough for five or even eight people, one could not just jump; it called for move-ment slow, dignified, composed; something not lightly to be undertaken, but a formal ceremony more impressive even than sitting down to a State Dinner.

By the side of the château is an old house, quaint, and a little tumbledown, which is known as the House of Rabelais. It could have been the Doctor's house, as far as age and situation are concerned, but there is no very good reason for thinking that it was, beyond the theory that there is usually some fire below a traditional smoke. Whether it was or not, Rabelais, one feels, belongs to Chinon, and not to Langeais.

A few miles on, Ussé provides as great a contrast to Langeais as does an Elizabethan courtier to a crusading knight. The first sight of it, all towers and chimneys and pointed roofs above a set of irregular, startlingly white, buildings quickens the breath of the least sensitive. It is lovely, but it has more prettiness and less beauty than Chenonceau. It is a fairy-story castle in real life; quite genuinely so, for this is the castle that inspired Perrault to write what is perhaps the best-loved, the most effective, the least likely to perish of all fairy-stories, save *Cinderella*, *The Sleeping Beauty*.

La Belle au Bois Dormant, the Beauty in the Sleeping Wood, is the French title. The dark background of trees, against which the white of Ussé is as clear and fair as the Princess's skin, the calm and many-towered château, the utter peace and silence of this little corner of Touraine between Indre and Loire, make the fairy-tale more real than historical events. Anything could happen here; what more probable than that within the great, deserted house there sleeps the most beautiful Princess in all the world? It is a setting fit for her, and for her alone. In the mind's eye, the bushes and the brambles grow and grow, covering all the lower windows. Nothing stirs, nothing will stir until the Prince arrives. Surely until now he never has, for had he awakened her with love's first kiss, the dream château must have dissolved into a nothingness. No other conclusion would be artistically satisfying.

As it is still there, so must the Princess be, still waiting for the perfect Prince to awaken her. The customary end of the story is a fabrication, a contrived happy ending to content the inmates of the nursery, a modern innovation. In fact the Princess still sleeps within the château, jealously guarded, and that is why the visitor is admitted to the little Renaissance chapel in the park, but not to the château itself. The latter he must admire from afar.

How much better that it should be that way. What could there be within that would not disappoint? The round white towers, holding, more than reflecting, the sunshine, for all their solidity are insubstantial as a dream. If Ussé has a history, if it were designed by human brain, built by human hands, I for one do not wish to know it.

The road that carries one reluctantly away from this brief return to childhood's fairyland runs south-east, parallel to the Loire; it passes through Rigny, which explains why in some reference books you will find Ussé indexed not under 'U' but under 'R' for Rigny-Ussé. Then it edges the forest of Chinon, turns sharply to the south and climbs on to the great wooded plateau, meets the direct, sunken road from Azay and Tours, and turns round the huge fortress, before giving the first view of the Vienne below. It is best to drive right round the outer fortifications and go to the bridge, in order to look up at Chinon as it ought to be seen, from the river.

The bridge follows the exact pattern of its predecessors (it is in fact built on twelfth-century foundations) and strides across the mid-stream island, on which, in 1321, all the Jews of the town to the number of 160, were burnt alive after being accused of poisoning the wells. This episode strikes the tragic note proper to the old town.

It is old, old, old is Chinon. In all its history there is

nothing but war and death and imprisonment. Only the
presence of Joan of Arc lightens for a few short days the
darkness of its story. The melancholy ruins of vast extent
have a tragic atmosphere still, of which even the least
sensitive are conscious. They cannot fail to impress, but
coming after the brightness of Ussé they impress with
sadness that so much effort and wealth and ingenuity
should have been expended upon a place that brought only
death and destruction and unhappiness.

The great plateau of Chinon across which our road has
run ends in a spur commanding the Vienne. From time
immemorial this spur has been a military post. It first
comes into recorded history as an *oppidum* of the Celts.
The Romans drove them out, and made there their own
castrum. If rather dubious records can be believed, Saint
Brice first built a Christian chapel there in the year 427.
Saint Mexme added a second, and then a monastery. The
chapel was enlarged to become a collegiate church in the
tenth century (it partly collapsed later, and is now a school).
Under Clovis, Chinon became the principal fortress of the
kingdom. It passed to the Counts of Blois, who held it in
the tenth and eleventh centuries, ceding it (1044) to Geoffroi
Martel, Count of Anjou. Thus it became the property of
that Angevin King of England, Henry II.

The fortress as we see it today is mainly the design, if
not the actual work, of Henry II. Originally it consisted of
two parts only, the Château du Coudray to the west and
the Château du Milieu, the Middle Castle. The third part,
the Fort of Saint George, now dismantled, was a postscript
dictated by experience. French efforts to reduce this English
stronghold demonstrated that whilst the river to the south
and the deep ravines to west and north gave protection
against sapping and mining, the Middle Castle was vulner-
able from the east. So Henry II built the new extension
and dedicated its chapel to the patron saint of England.

It was in the Fort of Saint George that Henry II died, and died badly, too, as the countryfolk still say in England, cursing his undutiful, ungrateful and rebellious sons, who were determined to enter into their patrimony before their father was dead. After lying in the chapel of Saint George, his body was transported to Fontevrault. His wife, Eleanor of Aquitaine, had retired to the convent there, where she died. Now they rest side by side in the abbatial church.

Their son, Richard Coeur-de-Lion, further strengthened the fortress and to good purpose, though not quite good enough. In 1204, Philippe-Auguste, King of France, laid siege to it in earnest.

As Henry II had foreseen, the eastern end proved the weakness, the only place where the walls could be sapped. For eight months according to some, for a full year according to others, the troops of Philippe-Auguste invested and assaulted. Time and time again the great timber-built mobile assault-towers were driven away from the walls. Then the walls of the Fort of Saint George were sapped, and the eastern defences fell. A deep ditch separated it from the Middle Castle (and still does, though it is now crossed by a stone bridge, replacing the ancient wooden draw-bridge), but proved ineffective. It was roofed over with stout timbers, and the sappers were able to continue their work almost unimpeded. Where the walls began to crack and split, as the mine collapsed after the wooden props had been set on fire, the huge mangonels would hurl their stones against them; then the battering-rams, sturdy tree trunks swung on ropes and chains from a triangulated framework and operated by as many as a hundred men at a time, would be brought in to complete the destruction. Such was the siege of Chinon; never again in its long history was it to be reduced.

Philippe-Auguste won his day, and from thenceforward Chinon remained not only French, but the main stronghold

of the French monarchy. To any but highly trained ob-
servers, the fortress today looks very much as it did in the
times immediately following the siege. The rocky platform
on which it is built, rising nearly 300 feet above the river,
shows clearly how the escarpment on the three sides was
cut away artificially so that the huge walls of smooth
masonry could be built in an unbroken vertical rise to the
top level of the cliff. They could not be sapped and, until
the invention of gunpowder, were unassailable. The remains
look perfect twelfth century; although the keep of the
Château du Coudray is reputedly the work of Philippe-
Auguste, there must be much doubt if any of the present
buildings are any earlier than the latter part of the fourteenth
or early part of the fifteenth century. There is one exception,
a round tower known as the Tour du Moulin, from having
once been surmounted by a windmill, which would seem
to be genuinely of the times of the Angevin Kings. To
most of us this will be a matter of complete indifference;
what is important is that we should be able from the present
ample remains to picture so clearly the events of 1204-5,
for later generations did no more than rebuild to the original
design of Henry II.

From the bridge across the river, the two remaining parts
of the fort, towering above the old houses and the narrow
streets and the twelfth-century parish church of Saint
Maurice, stand out against the skyline, grey and massive and
still evil. Across the bridge and up the hill are old streets,
so old that if any one house fell, surely all the rest would
come crashing down, too, like a house of cards. The tiny
mediæval square, the *Grand Carroi*, or Great Crossroads,
could hardly less deserve its description. Standing in it,
surrounded by the houses that have the very smell of
antiquity, it is not difficult to believe the legend that to the
one now used as a baker's shop Richard Coeur-de-Lion
was brought wounded from his disastrous attack upon

Châlus in the Limousin, and that there he breathed his last. Upon this mounting-block Joan of Arc stepped when, after all the frustration and delay, she was summoned to ride to the castle and meet the Dauphin. It is all age and peace and quietness until you raise your eyes and catch a glimpse of that sinister castle above you, and then the warmth goes out of the sunshine and the grey of the walls dims all the brightness of the day,

The entrance to the fortress is now at the south-east corner of the Middle Castle, by the stone bridge over the deep ditch (as already described, this separated the Middle Castle from the Fort of Saint George) and then under the narrow clock-tower. Only some sixteen feet wide for its height of nearly 120 feet, this tower looks from below to be no more than a narrow column. In a lantern on its platform hangs a great bell, once used for sounding the tocsin and now on more joyful local occasions.

It is the Middle Castle that was built on the site of the Roman *castrum*. The almost rectangular, long and narrow site is bounded by enclosing walls and converted, in these degenerate days, into the French conception of an English garden. Where once knights in armour tilted in dangerous exercise, where the bowmen perfected their aim, where the armourers made good the dents of battle, now blow the poppy and the rose. The Royal Apartments are no more than crumbling walls; they look over the town and the river.

Another deep ditch separates the Middle Castle from the Château du Coudray, including Philippe-Auguste's keep. The walls of the middle room of the keep are scratched with ancient graffiti, believed to be a reminder of another of Chinon's dark episodes, and the failure of a splendid ideal that after seven centuries still moves one to admiration. The story begins in 1119. Hughes de Payen, Geoffroi de Saint-Adhémer and seven other French knights bound themselves before the Patriarch of Jerusalem to guard pilgrims to the Holy Places from the attacks of the Saracens and took vows of chastity, poverty and obedience. They were given quarters close to the church of the Holy Sepulchre, on the site of the Temple of Solomon, from whence they took their title of Knights Templar. Saint Bernard of Clairvaux himself drew up the rules of their Order. Discipline was strict, the life austere; even the knightly pastime of hunting was limited to the chase of lion. No kiss of woman was allowed, not even of mother or sister. In the extraordinary climate of the time of the Crusades, the greatest recorded period of idealism in the history of the human race, the order swelled to huge numbers. By the year 1260 the Knights alone numbered 20,000, without taking into account the serving brothers. In all, over the years, 20,000 Templars perished for their cause in Palestine; the world has never known better soldiers nor men of higher courage against impossible odds. But the passionate faith of the Crusades died; battle by battle, the Holy Land and its approaches were lost. The Order retired to Cyprus, then to Tortosa, as the thirteenth became the fourteenth century. The Order had become rich and proud, servants of individual Popes rather than of the Church. It had entered into open warfare with the Knights Hospitaller, to the horror of good Christians everywhere. The wealth of the Templars became their downfall.

Philippe-le-Bel, Philip the Fair, of France at the beginning of the fourteenth century was a king who hid his vices and defects beneath the cloak of orthodoxy. The Pope, the miserable Clement V, was a creature of the King of France. The Templars were rich, the King was desperately in need of money. The Templars formed a State within the State; they paid no taxes, they obeyed only their own laws, they were a potential menace to the King.

In 1306, Clement V ordered the Grand Master, Jacques de Molay, to leave Cyprus, with the treasure of the Order, accompanied by all the high dignitaries, and to go to Paris. Estimates of their numbers vary greatly; 5,000 knights and 15,000 serving brothers is the highest. At the lowest computation, there were 1,500 knights, mainly French. Of these the principal ones, to the number of 140, took up residence with Jacques de Molay in their Temple in Paris.

On October 13, 1307, they were all seized, and carried to captivity in the strong towers of Chinon. There they lay imprisoned for years; there they had ample time to scratch upon the walls in the dismal light those messages of despair we still can see. Their chief fault had been arrogance, and that soon left them in their dark prison. It was not of that they were accused, but of such incredible sins as the denial of Christ, of spitting upon the Cross, of sorcery and Black Masses. Weak brethren were found to substantiate the charges; under weariness of the spirit from imprisonment, under weakness of the flesh from horrible tortures, many confessed.

Their confessions were not maintained on the scaffold. On May 12, 1310, after nearly three years of imprisonment, fifty-four of them were slowly burned alive; but even in the midst of their most awful agonies they refused to make further perjured confessions and died proclaiming their innocence. It was not until March 19, 1314, that Jacques de Molay and the aged Geoffroi de Charnay, Master of Normandy, were brought from prison to receive judgment. They firmly proclaimed the innocence of the Order, and their own. On the same day they were slowly roasted to death, asserting even in their agony, that their previous confessions, wrung from them by torture, were untrue. Just before the end, according to an old tradition that cannot be proved or disproved, Jacques de Molay 'in a loud voice and firm, summoned the Pope and King Philippe to meet him at the Bar of Almighty God before the year were out'. In fact, both Pope and King died within the twelvemonth.

Only in France was the Order found guilty. Elsewhere, either it was completely vindicated, or the members were given a nominal penance and their property handed over to the Hospitallers after some provision had been made for their support. In England, in spite of all the pressure the Pope brought to bear, only the Grand Master suffered; he died in prison, maintaining his innocence. Yet it is not to be said that there is no justice in human affairs; Philippe-le-Bel profited but little, even for the short time he had still to live, from the Templars' fortune. Force of public opinion obliged him to relinquish a large part of his booty to other monastic orders.

The keep of the Château du Coudray contributes not a little to the grim atmosphere of Chinon, and it is a relief to come out of it into the air and sunlight, and to look upon the little cluster of trees which have sprung up in the midst of the towers. Best of all is to go to the southern ramparts and to feast the eyes with the long vista up and down the valley of the Vienne.

The clear waters of the river sparkle and glisten between green meadows, and the shadows of poplars and walnut trees do not obscure them but merely accentuate their irridescence. As far as the eye can see there is nothing but greenery, meadowland, and clusters of trees, and vineyards. There is nothing to be seen but the useful product of man's labour, the raising and garnering of the fruits of the earth, the little houses to which generations of children have brought joy.

Only when the spirit has been refreshed by this lovely and tranquil scene can one properly be prepared to return to the gaunt ruins of the castle for its memories of Joan of Arc, and to the little town for the echo of the laughter of Rabelais.

CHAPTER XIII

The Maid

(*CHINON*)

IT was on March 4, 1429 that, on the tenth day of her journey from Vaucouleurs, Joan of Arc, clad in a man's black tunic and with boots, spurs and sword, arrived at Sainte-Catherine-de-Fierbois. There she heard Mass three times in the same day, and still found time to write to the Dauphin. She had travelled, she told him, 150 leagues to come to his help; she knew many things to his good, and would be able to recognise him amongst many others. In this letter we can see the beginning of the celebrated episode at Chinon.

Two days later she reached the end of her long journey, thankful to have escaped her Prince's enemies and to have been less delayed by the flooding rivers than had at first seemed probable. She lodged, by tradition, in an inn at the Grand Carroi, where she 'fasted and prayed'. This may be doubted; her own account is that she 'lodged with a good woman, near to the castle', which does not sound like an inn.

Her presence was announced to the Dauphin; he roused himself from his lethargy enough to send messengers to her, asking that she should declare her mission. At first she repudiated them entirely; her mission was to the Dauphin, and to the Dauphin only, and there could be no intermediary. The messengers came back again, with orders to explain to her that they were sent by the Dauphin in person, and that she need not hesitate to declare to them what she wanted with him. At length she consented to reply, telling them to inform their master that the King of Heaven had sent her with a double mission; first to raise the siege of Orleans, then to lead the Dauphin to Rheims for anointment.

After much dilly-dallying, Joan was sent for to the castle two days later. She mounted her horse and made her way up the hill as the visitor does today, crossed the drawbridge, and passed under the clock-tower to reach the Middle Castle. The story is told that as she was about to enter the castle a man on horseback called out to the people around, with a dirty laugh, '*Jarnidieu* (*je renie Dieu*, I deny God) is that not the Maid? If I could have her for one night, I would not return her in like condition.'

Joan turned round so as to look him in the face. 'Ha, in the name of God, you deny Him, and you so near your death?' The tale draws to an end like one of those moral stories which were the only permitted Sunday-reading of our more strictly brought up parents or grandparents. Within an hour the blasphemer had fallen into the river, and was drowned.

Of the great hall, the *Grande Salle*, which was then over 70 feet long and 25 feet wide, there now remains in the Middle Castle little more than a few steps leading to it, and the western embrasure with its wide fireplace; yet these trifling pieces are amongst the most evocative that all this land has to offer. With these in sight on the upper floor, it is easy to reconstruct in the mind the entire hall with its vast hooded fireplace, the three large windows overlooking the inner courtyard, and the smaller ones opening out over town and river.

Remembering the wording of her letter, the Dauphin had dressed less conspicuously than the gentlemen of his

Court, and hung back behind them to put her to her first test. Joan looked around her, and at first failed to find the person she had come to seek, whose description she must have asked for, time and time again during her journey, to be so certain of being able to recognise him when the moment came. She demanded indignantly that the courtiers should not seek to mislead her, and made her way through the crowd to the one she was seeking. The hall was lit by fifty torches, and over 300 people had crowded into it to witness the meeting of this strange, bucolic, self-styled messenger of God with their lazy almost-king.

'Gentle Dauphin,' she said, 'I am called Joan the Maid. The King of Heaven sends me to you with the message that you shall be anointed and crowned in the city of Rheims, and that you shall be the Lieutenant of the King of Heaven, who is the King of France.'

The Dauphin denied that he was the one she should be addressing. 'It is not I who am the King, Jehanne. There is the King.' Joan brushed aside this denial. 'In God's name, noble Prince, it is you and none other.'

With this the Dauphin drew her out of earshot of the others, and the conversation was continued privately. Yet, when the time came for the rehabilitation of Joan, the anonymous *Abbréviateur du Procès* was able to record it as if he had been present in person. Unfortunately we are not told what his authority was; perhaps the Dauphin confided it verbatim to some of his friends, or to his confessor. It is so detailed that, if it be true at all, it is a remarkable piece of memorising.

Joan began, according to this version, by reminding the Dauphin of some things that only he in the whole world could know. 'Sire, if I tell you things so secret that you and God alone are privy to them, will you believe that I am sent by God?' On the Dauphin agreeing, she continued. 'Sire, do you not remember that on last All Souls'

Day, being alone in your oratory in the chapel of the castle of Loches, you requested three things of God?'

'I remember it well,' replied the Dauphin.

'Have you ever spoken of these things to your confessor, or to any other?'

The Dauphin replied that he had not. If he were speaking the truth about this, it makes it the more unlikely that he reported the entire present conversation to his confessor, who might not have been pleased at not having been informed of the previous matters.

'Your first request,' Joan went on, 'was that it should be God's pleasure to remove your courage in the matter of recovering France, if you were not the true heir . . .'

This becomes understandable only if it is remembered that Charles' mother, the slightly mad Isabel of Bavaria, whose eleventh child and fifth son he was, indignantly denied that the late King Charles VI was the boy's father. With his own mother loudly proclaiming his bastardy, Charles VII may be excused for having some personal doubt as to the right by which he held the throne of France. Once he had become firmly established as the King of France, it became important to him and his children that there should be no doubt in the minds of his people about his birth; this part of the conversation, however much we may wish to believe the rest, must therefore almost certainly be apocryphal.

'. . . If you were not the true heir,' continued Joan, 'so that you should no longer be the cause of prolonging a war bringing so much suffering in its train.'

From all that is known of the character of Charles VII, this noble sentiment seems unlikely.

'The second request was that you alone should be punished, either through death or any other penance, if the adversities and tribulations which the poor people of France had endured for so long were due to your own sins.'

It is no insult to the memory of Charles VII to add that worrying about the adversities and tribulations of the poor people of France was not a prominent characteristic of the Valois Kings.

'The third request,' concluded Joan, 'was that the people should be forgiven and God's anger appeased, if the sins of the people were the cause of their trouble.' The Dauphin brought this conversation to an end by telling Joan, 'you have spoken the truth.'

There is better, and contemporary, authority for stating that in fact the Dauphin was so much in doubt still about Joan after their first meeting that she was lodged in the tower of the Château du Coudray, only after Madame de Trèves and Madame de Gaucourt had examined her and confirmed her sex. Up to that point, the Dauphin was still uncertain whether or not he was being hoaxed by a boy pretending to be a girl.

Still looked upon with suspicion and uncertainty, Joan's next days at Chinon can hardly have been happy ones. She was virtually a prisoner in the tower, with its single circular room on every floor, to which a little chapel was attached for her to pray. She was given a page to attend to her during the day, one Minguet de Contes, who seems to have been a devoted little servant to her. If only he had had a literary gift, what a remarkable eye-witness account of Joan's greatest days might we not have had from him; alas, he turned out to be a good soldier and nothing more.

With the arrival of the Dauphin's cousin, the Duke of Alençon, things looked brighter for Joan. It does not appear as though he believed in her mission, but it is clear that he liked her for herself. He whisked her off to Saint-Florent for a few days, to stay with his wife, which relieved Joan of the nightly presence of a woman who, for all her being of gentle birth, was no more than a gaoler.

When the men at Saint-Florent went tilting in the

19. MONTSOREAU. 'The château of the fifteenth century has some beautiful stone mouldings and arabesques.'

20. FONTEVRAULT. *'Under this strange, artistic and unique shape ar*
hidden five enormous openings for wood fires and no less than twent
chimneys.'

meadows, Joan insisted on accompanying them. To their great surprise, the sturdy country girl acquitted herself extremely well. As a token of his surprise and admiration, the Duke presented her with a horse.

Dates now become uncertain, for part of the written evidence that might have helped her at her trial would seem to have been deliberately suppressed. Her stay at Chinon would appear to have lasted into March, and from Chinon she went to Poitiers. It was there, and not after the first interview at Chinon, that Joan won recognition. She was examined by learned doctors, and perpetually at her trial called for 'the book of Poitiers' to be produced, but it never was. Later Frère Séguin, one of the examiners, recorded that 'we decided, in view of the imminent necessity and of the danger of Orleans, the King might allow the girl to help him and might send her to Orleans.' No great enthusiasm, even then; but better than the half-imprisonment that was her fate at Chinon. As we know, it was not until the very end of April that she finally got her wish to take part in the relief of Orleans.

Chinon then, though the brighter for the remembrance of the single-minded girl, was not a place that brought her any happiness beyond the transient satisfaction of meeting the Dauphin face to face. The Tour du Coudray still has about it a certain unhappy atmosphere as if the impatience and unhappiness of Joan had left an intangible but permanent record. Yet Joan did have her one brief moment of triumph within these walls. When she had passed all the tests, when she had reluctantly been accepted as the last hope of saving Orleans, she came back to Chinon. Whatever doubts those in authority might have had about her, the people, and the men-at-arms in particular, had none. Her piety, her complete confidence in the heavenly powers that would bring her mission to its predestined end, her gift of good-humoured but devastating repartee, had completely

N

convinced the simpler people. They accepted her at her own valuing, as 'one sent by God'. At Chinon she was equipped with her armour, provided with attendants; with her new banner flying, with the sword she had demanded from the church at Sainte-Catherine-de-Fierbois, she set out on April 20 towards her first and final triumph.

With her departure, the history of Chinon loses most of its interest. Only once more does it shine in any glory, although it remained the favourite residence of the Court until 1450. It remained unoccupied until the fifteenth century was drawing to a close. In 1498 Charles VIII died, and the crown passed to a distant cousin, a Valois-Orleans, known to us as Louis XII. In his will Charles VIII made it a condition of kingship that his successor should marry the widowed Queen, Anne of Brittany. Louis was already married, as you have read, to the pitiful, unattractive Jeanne de France. The Pope must be consulted: be made to see that reasons of State made it essential for Louis to obtain a divorce.

The Pope's reply was brought to Chinon by a distinguished Legate, Caesar Borgia. The castle was put *en fête*. The grey walls were hidden behind countless bright tapestries; thousands of torches brightened it by night; music was heard from every corner. In spite of all this, in spite of the throng of gaily dressed courtiers, each with a fortune in silk and brocade and gold and jewels upon his person, Caesar must have found it a dull and uninspiring setting after the Italy which was now burgeoning with the Renaissance.

The Papal Bull was read, the divorce declared. Poor Jeanne, who had been married to Louis to ensure that the daughter of France should be Queen of France, was Queen no more. Then Louis turned from the poor, deformed creature to wed the widowed Anne of Brittany, a marriage as much of inclination as of statecraft. It ensured the permanent inclusion of Brittany in the realm of France; it gave the new King of France a consort worthy of the country. When the festivities were over, Chinon was plunged into the obscurity in which we see it today.

Richelieu saw it, wanted it and, with no little trouble, got possession of it. Having got it, he did nothing with it. It remained in his family until the Revolution, falling to pieces a little more every year. It takes a long time for a mediæval stronghold to collapse, but the work of time is no less sure than the work of explosives. It would have been doomed to the same fate as Richard Coeur-de-Lion's other great castle, Château Gaillard, now no more than a ground plan and a few crumbling walls, if in our own time measures had not been taken to preserve what remained. At least further decline has been arrested, and now, very slowly, restoration is being carried out.

Oppressive as is the atmosphere of Chinon castle, it should be visited. Its sombre story is the prelude to the Renaissance. It is one of the few records in stone of that appalling period between the last efflorescence of Christianity in Europe and the first blossoming of the Continent's greatest artistic springtime. Against this stark backcloth the worst excesses of the Renaissance seem the less black, and the achievements shine with a greater brightness.

Nevertheless, it is a relief to pass out under the clock-tower and find ourselves again in the narrow streets of old Chinon. Between the wars, but I think no longer, the Renaissance house that stands on the corner of the Rue de la Lamproie was supposed to be that of Chinon's one great son, François Rabelais. The authorities decided that it was not, but that the true house of Rabelais once stood where number 15 is now, and fixed a plaque there accordingly. The old house has long since gone. It had been made into an inn, long after Rabelais' death, and prospered mightily from its connection with a man who had so whole-heartedly sung the praises of good food and good drink. Why it disappeared eventually, I cannot find out.

Was Rabelais born there? The general opinion is that he was not, that his birth was in that tiny family property, La Devinière, which has now become a Rabelais Museum. Certainly he came early to live in the family house at Chinon, where his father pleaded in the local court, and left it only to pursue his studies.

His work is full of Chinon and the locality; the shadow of the castle weighed not at all upon his high good humour. At Gargantua's birth feast was not the cry 'O *lacryma Christi*, it is the wine of La Devinière, it is of the finest grape'? The scene of the Picrocholian War is this countryside, and the 'cities' are the hamlets with which his boyhood had made him familiar. It is believed that he never in his life returned again to Chinon; but Chinon had formed him and Chinon went with him always to his last days.

His life is soon told, so few are the actual details recorded, and explains the man not at all. Even the date of his birth is an assumption; it must be placed between 1490 and 1494. His father combined his duties as a lawyer (the race that Rabelais mocked at every opportunity) with ownership of a few small properties around, including vineyards, which seem to have been let out on the *métairie* system, an old form of share-cropping still popular in France. Obviously there was not enough money to set up a younger son, so from the first he was destined for the Church. The Benedictines of Seuilly first educated him; then the Franciscans, at La Baumette, nearer to Angers. Finally the Friars of Fontenay, on the edge of the wild country of the Vendée, took him in hand. He read hard, but he read what he wanted: law and astronomy and the classic tongues, rather than the things of the Church that he should have been ingrossed in. He took Holy Orders and became a Franciscan.

The Franciscans displeased him very much indeed, and

through a friendship he had struck up with the young bishop of Maillezais, he got Papal dispensation to join the Benedictines. In the end they pleased him no better. Off he went to Montpellier to take a degree in medicine. He seems to have been there some years and, in addition to having a riotous time, on the evidence of his books, established a good practice and made some reputation for himself. He must at some time have been in contact there with that other extraordinary doctor, Nostradamus, but neither, in their written works, makes any reference to the other. The mystic Jew and the laughter-provoking Chinonnais were hardly likely to become great friends, but it would have been fascinating to know what one thought of the other.

In 1532 we find one of the few definite dates of his life. In that year he was attached to the hospital, the *Hôtel-Dieu*, at Lyons, and in the next three years published two very dull, sober and scientific medical works, and then *Pantagruel* and *Gargantua*. Cardinal Jean du Bellay has been noted before as the lover of poets and writers in general, which alone accounts for the presence of Rabelais in his suite at Rome in 1534. This little excursion was evidently undertaken without authority; for on his return in 1535, he was dismissed from the hospital for absence without leave. Back he went to Rome, persuaded Pope Paul III to release him from his monastic vows, which he never seems to have taken very seriously, and to grant him a licence to practise medicine. In the next two years, Paris, Montpellier and Lyons all saw him. Guillaume du Bellay appointed him his physician in 1539, and presented him with a living. The Third and Fourth Books of *Pantagruel* were published in 1546 and 1547, the former being privileged by the King. When François I fell ill in the latter year, Rabelais took time by the forelock and retired to Metz to be out of reach of the Sorbonne, who, not unnaturally after his virulent satires on that august body, were only prevented by the

King himself from attacking him. He returned to Rome
with Cardinal du Bellay; he was given the living of Meudon,
and, the year after the publication of the last part of the
Fourth Book, presumably died. At least no further record of
his being alive is to be found.

The mystery of Rabelais, in birth, in death and in his
work, becomes only the more profound as the years pass,
and so is that of his reputation. His name is universally
known; the names of his invented characters have passed
into almost every European language; yet the number of
people who have actually read *Gargantua* and *Pantagruel*
must be remarkably small. Everything is contradictory:
Mr. D. B. Wyndham Lewis maintains that he never resided
in his parish of Meudon; Sir Walter Besant described him
as growing old, living quietly at his *cure* at Meudon; according to some authorities he was born in 1483, others put it
as late as 1494. When so little is known for certain, surmise
can have a field day.

What is certain is that he formed friendships with the boys
of the great du Bellay family with whom he was at school.
These great patrons of literature in their later years would
not have been likely to extend their friendship to the middle-
class Rabelais, had he not been gifted in the things that
interested them. But why then did a boy devoted to literature become a novice in the Franciscan order, which
deprecated learning? The Besant theory is that no other
monastery would have him; but this is contradicted by the
fact that he had no difficulty in transferring later to the
Benedictines, a much more suitable order had he not
despised all monks quite so thoroughly. No, we must be
content to leave Rabelais, the man, as a mystery, and to
accept only that he lived and that he made the Renaissance
laugh, and squirm.

Gargantua the Giant is far older than Rabelais; for generations before his time all the dolmens in the Loire valley

were attributed to the giant's hand. The foundations of the
two books are in the folklore of Touraine. On to these folk-
tales Rabelais embroidered satirical scenes of all the life of
the Renaissance. The fat-living, idle, good-for-nothing
monks were his principal target, followed closely by the
narrow-minded doctors of the Sorbonne, the too-sectarian
reformers, the lawyers, the pompous, the would-be clever.
Entertaining as is all this satire, it alone would not have
given the books their lasting reputation. Throughout them
runs a vein of schoolboy humour, dirt and coarseness that
makes the reading of them today one perpetual wonderment
that François Rabelais should have dared to dedicate Book
III to the Spirit of the Queen of Navarre, that patron of the
arts, that great and gracious Lady.

But the very religious Margaret of Navarre, the
courageous defender of the Reformers even against her
beloved brother, François I, was herself the author of
the *Heptameron*, a pastiche of the *Decameron* of Boccaccio and
by no means Sunday School reading. To quote Mr. Wyndham Lewis, 'the dunghill is an integral part of the Renaissance *décor*, and the whole of the Renaissance is in Rabelais;
the intoxication of recaptured learning, the paganism of
the new philosophies, the restlessness, the dreams of
Columbus-voyages of the spirit, the red-hot appetites, the
cruelties.'

The cruelties, yes; again and again the modern reader
is brought up standing by some account in Rabelais of a
joyous adventure in which the fun is sheer cruelty—humour
on a level with that of the penny-dreadful. Such was the
Renaissance; like that were the people who built and dwelt
in these lovely buildings. Until we can laugh at the things
at which Rabelais meant us to laugh, we cannot begin to
understand the times or the people.

One thing that Rabelais did was enormously to expand
the French language; like our own Elizabethans, he col-

lected words as he went around and brought to French as then spoken a necessary addition of local words. He had no compunction also in inventing new Latinisms in French; there was more in him than intoxication of recaptured learning, there was also the intoxication of words.

It is customary to claim the translation of Rabelais into English by Sir Thomas Urquhart, and its completion by Peter le Motteux, as a masterpiece of its own, sacrosanct and not to be imitated. Because it would have been pedantic not to use a version already familiar to some readers, I have used it (with one exception) in the occasional quotations I have made from Rabelais' works, though with this generally held opinion I venture to differ. Theirs is not translation, it is a new version. Where the loquacious Rabelais uses a score of epithets to describe some unhappy character and, with considerable art, stops short of wearying the reader, Urquhart in his Scottish frenzy of mirth will find two score, and end by being a bore. Often (though le Motteux is more guilty of this than Urquhart) the sense of the French is not translated at all. However, I have an idea that if any man in our own times tried to publish a new translation of Rabelais, he would find himself in court on the grounds of printing indecent matter, so we shall have to put up for ever with what we have got in English, until we learn enough sixteenth-century French to read it in the original.

It is worth the effort of reading, and particularly prior to a visit of the châteaux; nothing else paints so well the moral background of the Renaissance. And I have an idea that if you sat long enough in the country inns around Chinon and listened to the frank conversation of the labourers, you would find many of Rabelais' jokes still in circulation, and much the same talk of vast meals, and of drinking bouts, and much the same praise of the product of the vine

—the vine which begins and ends the books of Rabelais and twists its tendrils into every page.

Perhaps, indeed, one should only read Rabelais when in Chinon, enjoying the sunshine of the Touraine, and mellowed by a good bottle of the wine of Chinon, or of Lerné, Ligré, Rivière, Cravant, Huismes or Beaumont. The broader jokes might seem much funnier then, the cruelty less reminiscent of our own cruel times.

CHAPTER XIV

From Prison to Choir School

(MONTSOREAU, FONTEVRAULT, TOURS)

THERE comes a time when the most faithful of wives, the most dutiful of sons, the most loyal of friends, refuse steadfastly even to contemplate looking at another château. That is the moment to take them to Fontevrault, rather on the principle of the old-fashioned sorbet, served in the middle of a banquet to cleanse the palate and whet the appetite for the next course.

From Chinon, the road runs westwards to join the Loire again; at Montsoreau a secondary road turns south to lead to Fontevrault, some three miles away. Only three miles, yet they suffice to ensure that one of the most interesting groups of buildings in the whole of the Loire valley remains unknown to the vast majority of those who speed along the highway.

It is a pity not to stop at Montsoreau. Exquisite little white wines come from the surrounding vineyards, and the château of the fifteenth century has one delightful pierced turret and some beautiful stone mouldings and arabesques. Its name brings to mind one of the lesser of Dumas' works, *La Dame de Montsoreau*, founded on the all-too-true story of that Jean de Chambes who, in the time of Charles IX, used the beauty of his wife, the Lady of Montsoreau, to snare and entrap Bussy d'Amboise, the Protestant

leader, whom he promptly assassinated. The murder did
not take place at Montsoreau, but at the Château de la
Coutancière, some ten miles north of Saumur, so that the
bloodstains are not upon this pretty little château, for which
one may be thankful.

Montsoreau, however, is just a turning point in the road.
Beyond lies Fontevrault, and a truly remarkable experience.
An abbey was built here towards the end of the eleventh
century. In 1119, the Pope himself consecrated the basilica.
The founder was a Breton priest, Robert d'Arbrissel, and
it was he who built the monastery and the nunnery, an
unusual combination in those days. Towards the end of
his life, he passed on his charge to the Abbess and not to
the Abbot, and Pétronille de Chemillé fulfilled her functions
so admirably that until the end of its days an Abbess always
ruled the twin establishments. Always favoured by the
Counts of Anjou, Fontevrault acquired a tremendous
reputation when the Counts became Kings of England.
Members of the most aristocratic families joined it; no
fewer than fourteen of the nuns who rose to become its
Abbesses were Princesses of the Blood Royal in their own
right.

Poor Fontevrault was pillaged twice, by the Huguenots
and by the Revolutionaries, but what is left is enough to give
a perfect idea of its huge size and importance in earlier
days.

It is as you approach the heavy entrance door that you
get your first surprise. It is a gaoler who opens it for you.
As he takes you round, there is a great noise of clattering
keys and the opening and closing of iron doors and gates.
Fontevrault is an Ancient Monument, fully protected by
the Beaux Arts. It is also a prison, and has been since 1804,
housing at times as many as 800 prisoners. The Beaux
Arts have managed to win back for themselves the abbatial
church, the refectory, the cloisters and the kitchens, and

these may be visited by all. Should you wish to see the
rest, you must obtain permission from the Minister of the
Interior, and he grants it rarely, and then only to men.
But even in the permitted parts, you may get occasional
glimpses of groups of prisoners. Your second surprise,
unless you are more accustomed to prisons than I am, will
be the monastic silence. It does not seem possible that
several hundred men, prisoners though they be, can make
so little stir.

The church is a splendid example of Romanesque; your
third surprise may well be to find the nave surmounted by
four cupolas, of the kind that are to be seen in Cahors and
Périgueux and Angoulême. For long, I was puzzled how
this almost Byzantine effect had found its way into this
part of France. I now know the answer as far as from the
Mediterranean to Angoulême, but I am still doubtful where
Fontevrault fits into the story.

In early days Montpellier was a great Mediterranean
port. Its University drew on all the sages of the Levant.
It became the great spice centre of the western Mediterranean (and still carries a pepper-pot on its arms). Here the
spice ships unloaded; as the increasing power and daring
of the Barbary pirates made the passage of the Straits of
Gibraltar too dangerous for merchant ships, spice caravans
were sent across France, to carry their wares to Paris and
the Low Countries and Germany and to the Channel
ports of England. The spice merchants established themselves in the towns that became stages on this route, and
where they settled they brought their own conception of
architecture from the East. It is not impossible that Fontevrault, even before there was an abbey there, was one of
these stages. It is more probable, though, that the same
architects and masons who built the cathedral at Angoulême
between 1110 and 1128 were brought into build the abbatial
church of Fontevrault, of which at least the apsidal choir

is of this period, though the present nave belongs to the next century.

In this nave are the tombs of the Plantagenets. For those who have forgotten their early history of England, one of the Counts of Anjou married-off his fourteen-year-old son to the twenty-nine-year-old Matilda, grand-daughter of William the Conqueror, Duke of Normandy and King of England. The youngster, Geoffrey, handsome and not a little vain, used to set in his cap a sprig of broom, *genêt*, and the nickname *plante-genêt* stuck. Their son, Henry, married the divorced wife of Louis VII of France, Eleanor of Aquitaine. In his own right he controlled Anjou, Maine, the Touraine, Normandy; in his wife's, Poitou, Périgord, Limousin down to Gascony, with a feudal call on the lords of Auvergne and Toulouse. When, two years after his marriage, he came to the throne of England as Henry II, he was a much more powerful man, even in France itself, than the King of France, which gave rise to the centuries of warfare that lasted almost unbroken until the Renaissance.

The tombs are recumbent statues, undoubtedly contemporary portraits, of Henry II and Richard Coeur-de-Lion in their royal robes; of Eleanor of Aquitaine (or of Guienne, if you prefer it), respectively wife and mother, who withdrew to and died at Fontevrault; and of Isabella of Angoulême, wife of their other and worthless son, King John Lackland. The figure of Eleanor is in wood, and may well have been the funeral effigy; the others are in sandstone, and the fidelity with which the involved draping of their robes has been carried out is quite remarkable.

Richard, as one might expect, makes the most remarkable figure. If this be a portrait in stone, then he was indeed a fine figure of a man, some six feet six inches tall, broad-shouldered and broad-faced. The statues were mutilated at the time of the Revolution, not enough to deprive them of interest, but sufficient to dim what must have been striking likenesses. That perhaps is why it is difficult to see in this handsome warrior the undutiful son of the legend of Fontevrault.

Henry II, as mentioned in a previous chapter, died in the fort at Chinon, lay in the Chapel of Saint George, and was brought to rest at Fontevrault. Richard came to pay those respects to his corpse which were traditional. According to legend, the dead body shuddered convulsively and shed drops of blood all the time Richard stood before it; 'the very corpse,' in the words of the chronicler, 'as it were abhorring and accusing him of his unnatural conduct.'

The cloisters, the chapter house, the refectory are all large and gloomy and silent and depressing in their emptiness; but the kitchens provide the last, and a pleasant, surprise. The building is a strange octagon, half-towers at each corner with conical roofs, changing into an oblong in the central part, the roof ending as a pyramid. A thousand guesses as to its use would be unlikely to bring the right answer, for under this strange, artistic and unique shape are hidden five enormous openings for wood fires and no less than twenty chimneys. In fact the most modern hotel in the world has no better designed kitchens than these, the only ones of the Romanesque period that remain to us. Even when cooking for the several hundred inmates of the monastery and the nunnery with open wood fires, the heat would never have been intolerable, and there would have been no smoke and no danger from sparks. This astounding technical and artistic achievement cannot be less than eight hundred years old; nothing better of its kind has ever been done since.

With that sobering thought, let us continue on our road, back to the Loire, then across it, to turn north-eastwards on the last stage of the journey. This main road to Tours is not in itself either beautiful or interesting, but it does help the driver to cover the miles at good speed, provided always that he does not succumb to the temptation to turn aside to visit Cinq-Mars-la-Pile, a mysterious tower of the Gallo-Roman epoch ending in four pyramids, whose purpose and origin remain wrapt in mystery; or Luynes, a funereal feudal château of immense and depressing power; or Plessis-lès-Tours, where a few parts remain of the château of Louis XI so powerfully described in Sir Walter Scott's *Quentin Durward*.

Tours itself is a busy French provincial town, with wide avenues and some fine old buildings that have to be sought out. It must be considered disappointing in that so old and potentially interesting a place has been so greatly modernised. Heavy bombing in the last war did not help its appearance. But Tours is always worth a visit, if only from the fact that (may I be forgiven by the good people of some other towns in France I can think of) in my opinion it is easier to eat well there, within a wide price range, than anywhere else. It might be possible, after long search or just through sheer bad luck, to have a bad meal in Tours, but I doubt it.

Food is uniformly good in Touraine, and there are very few local specialities; the speciality of the Tourangeau is to cook straight-forward food exceedingly well. This, I am inclined to think, is a blessing. The 'local speciality' is being abused, being served to poor unsuspecting travellers who know no better, in season and out, often with ingredients imported from outside the region. There is nothing better than a local dish made from local produce at the time of year when it is at its best, but the 'regional speciality' in some parts is well on the way to becoming a racket and an excuse for high prices.

Rillions and *rillettes*, those delicious hors-d'oeuvres, made from fresh pork, shredded and prepared I know not how, are true local delicacies, and so are the cheeses, Olivet and Saint-Benoît, Valençay and Crémets (with which should be drunk the red wine of Bourgueil) but, at least with the womenfolk, the fame of Tours rests on its pastries, lighter and creamier than all others. They are not inexpensive; they could not be, when so much fresh butter and fresh cream go to their making.

Tours is the town of Saint Martin, the one, you will remember, who, when a Legionary in the Roman army of occupation, cut his cloak in two with his sword in order to give part of it to a shivering beggar. It was after this episode that he was baptised, and later became the greatest bishop of Gaul. He founded the first monastery to be built on the soil of Gaul. The people of Tours begged him to become their bishop. When he died at Candes in 397, they had to steal his body away from the monks of Poitou who wished to keep such holy relics. In 470, a magnificent basilica was built to honour his remains.

The first basilica was destroyed by the Normans. It was rebuilt, on a vast scale, between the eleventh and thirteenth centuries to meet the needs of countless pilgrims who came from every Christian land. It was sacked by the Huguenots in 1562, and fell to ruin thereafter. The remains of the nave were pulled down in 1802 to make way for a new street.

The present Tour Charlemagne and Tour de l'Horloge mark respectively the northern and the south-western limits of the old basilica; to walk from one to the other gives an idea of its once enormous size. The new Basilica occupies the site of part of the old east end, and the tomb of Saint Martin, which was under or near the altar of the old, is at the north end of the new. Only the cloisters of Saint Martin, which ran alongside and beyond the old south transept, remain of this fine old church, except of course the two towers mentioned above.

The Cathedral of Saint-Gatien gave rise to a popular
saying, 'as long as the building of Saint Maurice,' for until
the fifteenth century it was dedicated to Saint Maurice, and
took 327 years to build. Thus three phases of Gothic are
clearly to be seen in it: the east end, the early period; the
transept and the nave, the middle period; the façade, the
sad conclusion, when the purity of the Gothic theme disappeared beneath the flamboyance of an age that had
already forgotten the beginnings.

In its own way, the façade is very fine, and of extraordinary richness; it was built late, between 1426 and 1547,
so that it is not surprising that the two towers (dissimilar,
though this is difficult to spot at first) end in domes of pure
Renaissance design. Unfortunately, the façade was stripped
at the Revolution of nearly all its statues, and those that
can easily be seen from the ground are modern.

Once you step inside Saint-Gatien, the over-ornamented
front is forgotten in the glory of stained glass windows that
rival almost those of Chartres. Those of the radiating chapels
and the upper windows of the choir date from the thirteenth
century; the rose windows of the transept from the fourteenth; the great wheel of the nave from the fifteenth.
You may see in them the legend of Saint Thomas and Saint
Stephen, Saint Denis and Saint Vincent, the two Saints
John, Saint Peter and Saint Paul; you may see the Passion,
the Tree of Jesse, scenes from Genesis, and contemporary
workers in the fields. You can see them in such a blaze and
magnificence of colour as will fill your eyes and your heart
with delight, as perfect an example of the co-operation of
artist and artisan over a span of three hundred years as it is
possible to imagine. Miss anything else in Tours rather than
the windows of Saint-Gatien.

In the sixteenth century, Tours had 80,000 inhabitants;
in 1801 this figure had fallen to 20,000. The reason was to
be found in the Wars of Religion. Louis XI, who had a

o

sharp eye for business, tried to introduce the manufacture of
silk and cloth of gold in Lyons, but the Lyonnais at that
time had not seen the light and showed no enthusiasm at
all. The King moved the technical workers to Tours. By the
sixteenth century, the industry gave employment to 20,000
men. It was these men who flocked to the standard of
Reform. Protestant and Catholic waged bitter war in Tours.
Over the years, the workers drifted away from intolerance
of their faith; the great majority of them went to the Netherlands. The days of the prosperity of Tours were over. If the
population is now 80,000 once again, the reason is the
railway, whose works employ large numbers at nearby
Saint-Pierre-des-Corps.

On the whole, Tours has surprisingly little record of the
outstanding characters of the Renaissance who lived all
around and who must have frequented the only great town
in the immediate neighbourhood. South of the church of
Saint Julian (a thirteenth-century primitive ogival building
of some interest), is the Hôtel de Semblançay, the town
house of that unfortunate Treasurer of France whose fate
was described in the chapter on Chenonceau. There is the
Tour de Guise (now incorporated in the Meusnier Bar-
racks) much older than its name implies. It is, in fact, all
that remains of the original fort that Henry II of England
built to guard the passage of the river.

It was in this fort that the Dauphin first received Joan
of Arc, on May 14, 1429, after the relief of Orleans. She
had left Tours for Orleans on April 24, but there is no record
of where she stayed on the former occasion. The people of
Tours claim, with pride, that her standard and her armour
were the work of craftsmen of the town.

This, however, is far from explaining its present name:
Tour de Guise. It has already been told how, at Blois,
Duke Henri de Guise was assassinated on December 23,
1588, and his brother, the Cardinal of Lorraine, the follow-

ing day. There remained the son of the Duc de Guise, the Duc de Joinville. The King imprisoned him in this tower. The young Duke was not the man to wait for the problematical mercy of Henri III. With the help of friends outside and a bribable gaoler inside, he gradually had lengths of rope brought up to his room and with their aid escaped down the side of the tower. The Guise family being far more popular than the King, the tower has ever since been known by its present name.

In the cathedral, on the corner of the south transept, is the monument to the two children of Charles VIII and Anne of Brittany, but for whose untimely death there would have been no Valois-Orléans succession. They are rather touching, these figures of the two princes reclining on their tomb and watched over by angels. Had they lived, how different might have been the history of France; and Mary, Queen of Scots, would have been a poorer woman all her life. Touraine was the apanage granted to her on her marriage to the short-lived François II. Even whilst she was in captivity in England, she drew revenues from it as Duchess of Touraine.

The Porte Hugon in Tours is supposed to have given their name to the Huguenots, as being one of the favourite meeting-places of the Reformers, but this assumption must not be given a higher rating than 'not proven'. More vividly associated with them is the Rue Renard. During the religious riots in Tours, the Catholics would hunt down the Reformers with cries of the chase; *au reynard*, 'the fox is away', being the favourite. As the Rue Renard was on their route to safety amongst their own kind, it was there most often that they were overtaken and cut down.

There are other interesting things to see in Tours, from the lovely eighteenth-century, fifteen-arch bridge (which looks perfectly ridiculous in a dry summer, stretching out over a mere trickle of water), to the cloisters of La Psalette, or old Choir School; but I think as rewarding an occupation as any is to sit on a café terrace in the long and wide Rue Nationale, a continuation of the same bridge, and look around the skyline. Then you will understand why the town is called Tours, and why the towers still make up its coat of arms.

CHAPTER XV

The Beginning and the End

(CHAMBORD)

O N the last stage of the journey the road from Tours
to Blois is almost constantly in sight of the river.
It leads through Vouvray or, to be exact, it touches
a corner of Vouvray and then turns off to follow the river.
The wise traveller will carry on to the village, and later
rejoin the main road after a glance at the vineyards and the
cave-dwellings of Vernou. Here are the most famous vineyards for white wines in all Touraine, and not to drink a
bottle on the spot is almost a crime. At the end of the last
century, Vouvray proudly claimed of its wines that they
were 'the only ones able to be compared to Champagne',
and it is true that a good Vouvray is better than an indifferent Champagne. Wisely they have dropped the claim;
Vouvray can stand on its own feet and does not need the
adventitious support of the name of Champagne. It is not
and never can be a Champagne, but it is a fine sparkling
wine in its own right and with its own flavour.

Thereafter, from Blois to Mer is a route we have already
traversed; once across the river at Mer, D112 leads to
Chambord through the park. It is a Gargantua amongst
parks, now a game reserve, nearly 14,000 acres in area and
enclosed by the longest wall in France, 21 miles or so in
circumference. The six main alleys end in six sturdy gates.

Through one of these the visitor enters; there is a long

sandy drive, and then the sensational first view of the château. For a second or two the visitor seeing it for the first time just stands in disbelief.

My companion, the long-suffering owner of the car in which we travelled, is not a man given to strong language, but I am obliged to record that he fell from grace on this occasion. 'My God,' said he, 'What is that?' I had my answer ready in one of those impromptu phrases one has been longing to use for weeks.

'This,' said I, 'is the skyline of Constantinople on a single building.' I might have added that it is all the vigour and exuberance of the Renaissance carried to fantastic lengths, an example of the iniquitous folly of kings, a palace built at incredible cost in the midst of a desert when the Treasury was empty, the scene of the triumph of Molière that was almost a disaster. I might indeed have gone on for a long time, but it would have been trouble wasted, for my friend was beyond taking in anything but the sight that met his eyes.

Chambord is an oblong, about 170 yards long by 120 yards deep: its main features at the lower levels are six immense round towers, 60 feet in diameter, which seem an exaggeration of all the round towers one has seen on all the other châteaux. Except for the prodigious number of windows, for the châteaux has 440 rooms, the lower levels are sober and simple in design; just enormous, not ornate. But at roof level, Renaissance fantasy has burst into a flowering, tropical in its bewildering variety and richness of forms. There is the great lantern, the turrets, the dormers, the 365 chimneys, little cupolas, bells in stone, miniature steeples, and all the fantastic carving that came from a veritable explosion of creative energy. Fantastic is the only word for it, and the fantasy is successful. The product of this efflorescence ought, from its very exaggeration, to be in perfect bad taste; somehow, and I cannot explain it, it manages to produce this stunning effect and yet remains worthy of its era of good taste.

It is only as you approach and prepare to enter the 'court-yard of honour' that you realise there is a building within a building. Inside the outer oblong and forming an inner extension of the north-west façade, is a square building, with two more round towers of its own to match the two more central towers of the main frontage. Inside this keep is a staircase, *the* staircase, in the very centre of the square. It rivals that of Blois: if it could be seen from outside, it would surpass it. It is surrounded by four guard rooms, in the shape of a Greek cross; as originally designed, it reached in an unbroken spiral to the roof. The impression it gave must have been terrific, but unhappily such mundane concerns as draughts of almost gale strength made it neces-sary to diminish its appearance by inserting landings at the different floors.

The decoration is not so fine as that of Blois, but the conception even finer. It is a very beautiful double spiral, so contrived that different parties may pass up and down without ever meeting, and hardly seeing each other, except through the pierced stone-work of the central post. The double spiral rises to roof height; beyond that, a single spiral rises nearly another hundred feet into the superb lantern.

Even this magnificent creation of the early Renaissance is not the chief attraction of Chambord, though it would make the fortune of any other castle. Chambord's unique glory is the terrace along the roof. This was the grandstand for all the great events under the monarchy; here the Court spent most of its time in fine weather, watching for the King to return with his huntsmen, or looking down on military parades below, or tournaments, or dancing. In the intervals, or on the days (which were few when royalty was in residence) when there was nothing else to look at, time was passed most agreeably in examining all the wealth of carving and design. To note all the details might well take a month.

How did such a place ever come to be built in the midst of this sandy waste? And why this fantastic palace? Curiously enough, in an age which has left so many records, there are no certain answers to these two questions.

The Counts of Blois had always been great hunters, and, unattractive in many ways as was their great forest of Boulogne (for forest in its original meaning is more akin to heath than to woodland), it held more game than all their other possessions. It was a long way to Blois, twelve miles by the shortest route from the nearest point of the park, so they built themselves a hunting lodge where now stands the château.

In 1519, François I, possessor of their domain and no less a hunter than the Counts, knocked down the hunting lodge and began to build a palace for himself. It was a most unpromising site, with no proper road leading to it, surrounded by marshes and lacking every single advantage that an almost infinite number of riverside sites might have given him. Blois and Amboise, one would have thought, were near enough and big enough to give him all he wanted in size.

There are many theories, including one that he was carrying on a love affair with a lady living nearby, which is probable enough until one realises that there was no château nearby for the lady to live in. The other major theory is that it was just his passion for the chase. In the absence of all definite information, my theory is as worth considering as any other; I believe that it was the creative urge. François chose a desert site deliberately; he wished to make the wilderness flower. The greater the difficulties in his way, the greater his satisfaction in success. To have an army of workmen under his direction working to alter the face of nature, would satisfy his pride. Chambord, like Versailles, was the work of a megalomaniac.

Who designed this essay in exaggeration? Comparatively recent research has brought forward the name of Dominici de Cortone, probably one of the Italians whom François brought with him from his wars; however, at different times (it seems that an average of 1,800 men worked on it for fifteen years) other names appear, French names: Pierre Neveu, Denis Sourdeau, Jean Gobereau. The general intendant of the work was the Governor of Loches and Blois, François de Pontbriant. With the exception of de Cortone, who was one of the architects of the old Hôtel de Ville in Paris, none of these names have any significance today. There is a legend—it is hardly more than that— that François, passionately interested at that time in architecture, interfered so much with the architects that, one after the other, they refused to continue any longer and were either dismissed for contradicting the King or took themselves off elsewhere. According to this, François himself would be the true architect of Chambord, and, when it came to finishing the building, he is supposed to have called all the masons together and told each to do on the roof what he was best able to do, and to put the Italians to shame. So each master-mason went his own way and made his own designs. Hence the skyline of Constantinople.

At best this legend could only be a partial truth, for the staircase was no beginner's design, nor the great lantern, nor the Tower of the Fleur-de-Lys with the six-foot Lily of France that surmounts it. This Fleur-de-Lys escaped the first Revolution, but was dragged down in 1848, and replaced later.

Whoever the masons were, and whose-ever designs they worked to, they were good servants of the King. It is impossible to escape the King's salamander emblem anywhere; even the eight buttresses of the giant lantern are ornamented with colossal salamanders and the huge letter 'F' many times repeated.

The château is very empty today, and, if you stray away from the guide, you may well get lost in it; in addition to the great staircase, there are thirteen others hardly less imposing. There are no fires on a cold day in the 365 rooms, despite their chimney-pieces, so if you are to get lost in these, or in the 75 others without chimneys, it is best to choose a warm summer day for the adventure.

François, not the most consistent of men, pursued his building career at Chambord without interruption. When there was no money at all in the Treasury, when there was no money to ransom his two sons, who were prisoners in Spain, he still went on with Chambord. At one time he even considered altering the course of the Loire to make it run in front of the château, but the technicians refused to undertake such a task. If Leonardo da Vinci had been with the King at the time, how he would have enjoyed preparing plans for such a gigantic scheme. By the time he came, however, the little river Cosson had been turned from its bed to give the château its own stream instead. Originally the château was surrounded by moats, and was reflected at all angles in the still waters; but they were filled in, to the great loss of the château which had been designed with them in mind.

Chambord, as befits a building which looks the outcome of sheer high spirits, has no tragedy associated with it, unless one considers the death of that old reprobate, Maurice of Saxony, the Maréchal de Saxe, to fit that description. Chambord is associated almost entirely with solemn entrances, with all the gaiety of Court life, with the fun of the chase, and with a good deal of philandering.

The first great event at Chambord was in 1539, when François I received the Emperor Charles V there. As the Imperial visitor approached, he was waylaid by whole swarms of young women, all dressed (or undressed) as Greek goddesses. They ran in front of his horse, and strewed

his path with the flowers of Touraine. The grave Emperor
had no active dislike of being surrounded by pretty girls,
and was fascinated, as well he might be, by the appearance
of the château. When he had seen the great staircase, when
he had seen the rooms, not bare as they are now, but full
of fine furniture and handsome decorations, he turned to
his host and said, 'Chambord is the epitome of human
industry.' We may be sure that his keen eye did not miss
what has been described as 'a courtier's summary of the
King's existence', the dainty Love chasing a salamander in
a niche of the staircase.

There is a famous later memory of François. You will be
reminded of it by the guide when you are taken to what
used to be the King's Cabinet, which a Polish king who was
a later tenant most unfittingly turned into an oratory. Here
you will be shown the pane on which he wrote with his
diamond ring the regretful words which summed up the
wasted years, *Souvent femme varie, fol qui s'y fie*, or, according
to another version, *Toute femme varie, mal habile qui s'y
fie*, but the sense is the same in both: 'Woman is fickle,
it is madness to trust her.'

There is something just a little sad in the picture of the
now coarsened monarch, a martyr to internal ulcers, as
near heart-broken as so selfish a man could be from finding
that his mistress, the Duchesse d'Etampes, was conspiring
against him. The days when he had been the Cavalier-King,
slim, handsome, almost irresistible to women, were far in a
past to which there was no return. At least he had the satisfaction of knowing that if any man had the right to speak
of women from long and intimate experience, it was he
himself.

Henri II continued the building of Chambord, which was
still not complete at the death of François. Once at least
during his reign, it was the scene of an event in international
history when, in 1552, the German Princes came to sign

the treaty which drew within the boundaries of France the bishoprics of Metz, Toul and Verdun. Henri did not think that Germans, even princely Germans, warranted any more Greek goddesses; Chambord on that occasion was the scene of military parades, almost equally picturesque, with silk coats and velvet hats and multi-coloured plumes.

In due course François II and Charles IX came to Chambord for the hunting, and the great château was filled with the noise of their gay, young Courts, when 'the chatter of the girls and the singing of the men were as loud as the baying of the hounds'. The staircase proved a godsend to the minxes; could it have been designed for that purpose? They ran away from their admirers, up and down the staircase, allowing just fleeting glimpses to be caught through the open spaces of the pillar, and on it no lover could catch his lass unless she intended him to, with every protestation, doubtless, of its being unwished.

Chambord did not see the royal family again until the time of Louis XIII, and then he passed it on to his unworthy brother, Gaston d'Orléans, as part of the County of Blois which, as you have already read, the King gave to Gaston to keep him out of mischief and away from Paris and his conspiracies. The only memory that Gaston has left at Chambord is, a little unexpectedly, a family one. His young daughter, the *Grande Mademoiselle*, used to forget her dignity and his in playing with her father, more innocently, the staircase game of the loving couples of earlier reigns.

Louis XIV loved Chambord, in which is to be found the germ of Versailles. Versailles was built in the heart of an even greater wilderness than Chambord; Versailles called for even more water to be brought from even greater distances; Versailles overshadowed Chambord in size, as Chambord did all other new châteaux of its times.

Louis would arrive with a procession of cavaliers and

litters that stretched for miles. He was obliged to make considerable alterations internally to house this tremendous suite. And amongst other additions, he built a stage in one of the four guard rooms round the great staircase.

It was in this room in the year 1669, that Molière gave the first performance of *Monsieur de Pourceaugnac*. With his heart in his mouth, he watched the King's face for laughter. The King did not laugh; as the King did not laugh, no courtier dared to laugh. The comedy was played to a deathly silence; not even Lulli's music caused a single hand to beat against another in applause. Lulli himself, so goes the story, saved the day. He was playing the part of the Apothecary. In despair at the frigid reception of his friend's play, he risked everything, jumped from the stage, feet together; landed on the accompanist's harpischord; and went right through it. The bored King roared with laughter, and all his Court with him. The ice was broken; the King went on laughing for the rest of the play; and Molière's creation, hastily written in a few days at the château itself, was everywhere pronounced a prodigious success.

Once more, the following year, was Molière to face initial disaster and final triumph at Chambord. This time it was the first performance of *Le Bourgeois Gentilhomme*, and Molière had good reason for fright. If the King approved, all would be well; but if the King did not, Molière was in for a very bad time from the Court, for his comedies did not spare the courtiers and gentlemen.

During the first act, the King was as glum as a mute at a funeral; already the courtiers were exchanging glances, and metaphorically rubbing their hands and preparing the shafts of sarcasm they would hurl at the unhappy author. Right to the end of the play, the King still said nothing either to praise or to dispraise, and the gentlemen of the Court were left still undecided which way to jump. They would probably have given rein to their feelings, had not the King agreed to a second night. When the play was put on again, the King showed and said that he greatly enjoyed it; the courtiers swallowed their pride, and praised the author.

There are those who claim that *Le Bourgeois Gentilhomme*, laughing at the gentlemen as well as at those aping them, was the first step towards the Revolution. What Molière began, Beaumarchais with his *Figaro*, Voltaire, and a thousand other lesser spirits, completed. To this day, in France, irony is deadlier than any physical weapon.

In the next reign, with Versailles to occupy his thoughts, Louis XV had no further need of Chambord, and presented it to his father-in-law, Stanislas Leczinski, King of Poland, who occupied it from 1725 to 1733. Here he spent much of his time in prayer and in bemoaning the kingdom of which he had been deprived. He turned the King's Cabinet of the days of François I into his oratory; he also had the moats filled in. Beyond these two unfortunate occurrences, his eight years at Chambord were without note.

He was succeeded, in 1748, by the greatest character of them all, the Maréchal de Saxe. The gift to him of Chambord, with an annual grant of 40,000 *livres* to sustain it, was so ironic that it can hardly have been unintentional. Maurice of Saxony, Maréchal de Saxe, the hero of that Pyrrhic victory at Fontenoy for which this gift was a reward, was none other than the bastard son of Augustus of Poland who had chased Stanislas off the throne.

The old Marshal lived in state at Chambord. With him he brought six cannon taken from the enemy in battle, and two regiments of cavalry whom he used to review from the terrace, though barely able to stand. Discipline was rigid, and from time to time some military delinquent was to be found hanging from one of the neighbouring trees to encourage his fellow cavalrymen to behave better. This stern disciplinary measure was more reasonable than might appear at first sight, for the tough old warrior had chosen his regiments from Cossacks and Tartars and Wallachians, and even a handful of Martinique negroes, more accustomed to murder and pillage than to a peaceful life. They were all mounted on wiry little horses from the Ukraine, which were allowed to roam free and forage for themselves in the forest; when they were needed for dressing or parade they were summoned by a trumpet call, and were so well trained that they came of their own accord.

The fierce old soldier was not the man, and never had been, to allow a military life to occupy all his time. He had a passion for the arts, when the arts were represented by comely actresses. Already, nearly twenty years before, his name had been bandied about in connection with Adrienne Lecouvreur, the supreme actress of the Comédie Française, the idol of Paris playgoers. She died, suddenly and horribly, of poison. Some said it was self-administered, and that she took it because her heart was broken by Maurice of Saxony. Others maintained that she had been poisoned by a rival, who found himself supplanted by Maurice. The truth lies hidden. It was only in 1952 that workmen digging in a Paris street came across her remains; she had been refused Christian burial, and was interred at the foot of her own garden. The grave had been forgotten; the city had taken part of the garden for road widening. For nearly two centuries, the people of Paris had been treading over her grave, unaware.

Now another famous actress, La Favart, was brought to Chambord, more, it would appear, by sheer terror than by love of the old tartar. Maurice got himself busy, and Molière's stage was brought into use once more. On the platform from which a Lulli had once jumped and on which a Molière had played with his heart in his mouth, La Favart declaimed to the decrepit Marshal. Her husband was author, producer and stage manager of the little pieces in which she played. Unhappily none of them have survived to show the Marshal's tastes.

In due course, at the end of 54 years of an extremely well-filled life, Maurice died. In accordance with his will, for sixteen days the six cannon 'taken from the enemy in action' fired a mourning salvo every quarter of an hour. According to one account, he was mortally wounded in a duel by the Prince de Conti, who was defending his wife's honour.

The great days of Chambord were drawing to a close. It was gutted at the Revolution. In 1809, it was presented by Napoleon to Berthier, Prince of Wagram, who sold the timber and never lived there. His widow put the entire property up for sale; it was purchased by public subscription and presented in 1826 to the Duke of Bordeaux, the posthumous infant son of the Duc de Berry, and heir to the throne. This aroused the most violent feelings in France, and the echoes of the argument have not so long since died away. Fifty years later, the Duke came near to being made Henri V of France, but the proposal fell through. Chambord passed to two of his nephews; their heirs fought a long legal battle for possession of it. The State finally bought it in 1932 for eleven million francs.

At the end of all this petty wrangling, Chambord was to know one more glorious day, and to be saved by a man of noble character. It was August 21, 1944. The Germans, angry at the defeat they were suffering at the hands of the Allies, were about to burn the château, on the pretext that shots had been fired at them from the roof. This would have been a tragedy far surpassing the loss even of a Chambord, for in it were stored priceless works of art from many French national museums.

With great personal courage, Canon Gilg, the *curé* of Chambord, intervened. None will know now with what reasons, with what arguments, he won the day, but he succeeded in spite of the fact that, as an Alsatian of nearly 80 years of age who had once been, from their point of view, a German, he was not likely to be in German good graces. There must have been about him something of the air of an Old Testament prophet, of a man who has talked with God; for not only was the château and its treasures spared, but the hostages, who were momentarily expecting death, were released, as well as some of the men who had gone 'underground' and had been caught. There could be no more fitting episode on which to end an historical survey of Chambord.

The furnishings of the château are of an almost staggering banality. Many of them relate to the little Duke for whom it was bought by public subscription: a toy battery of artillery, working miniatures for the boy to play with, but which, as they needed gunpowder, he was not allowed to have. There are the coaches which the Royalists presented to him in 1873, when it seemed certain that he would become King, and which were never used for that triumphal entrance into Paris, and the tapestries that the ladies of Poitou gave him a few years later, all in the worst of taste.

The pictures are quite interesting: Turenne, Condé, Racine, Louis XIV and Maria Leczinska. The authenticity of most of them is extremely dubious, but there is a fine and genuine Clouet portrait of Henri III. There is no picture of Maurice of Saxony; instead there is an enormous earthenware stove he brought with him, and the very anonymous marble table on which he was embalmed. The only relic that moves one at all is in the old chapel, a tapestry woven by the little Madame Royale in the prison of the Temple, in Paris, from which her father, Louis XVI, and her mother were taken to the scaffold.

I mention these to support my contention that it were better by far to leave these châteaux entirely unfurnished, rather than to spoil the vision, that each one can create

P

for himself, of how these splendid rooms would have looked in their heyday. Many of the objects now to be seen in them are quite unworthy of their setting; they would have been thrown out in disgust by the original creators of the buildings. Chambord in particular suffers in this respect.

As we left Chambord, the workmen were already busy checking the installation that, when darkness fell, would flood the château with artificial light and set the sleepy birds and squirrels chattering at the noise of broadcast sound echoing in park and gardens. Twice that evening would the crowds troop in to see the floodlit building and to hear the amplified commentary. Night would bring no peace to Chambord.

Adieu, fantômes.

'SPECTACLES DE SON ET DE LUMIÈRE'

THERE has been a new development in recent times. In order to raise funds for the preservation of the châteaux, some are flood-lit by night all through the summer and, twice or three times between the fall of darkness and midnight, commentaries are broadcast from loudspeakers concealed in trees and bushes. Leading French actors and actresses have recorded for them little speeches, supposedly those of the characters who have played their part in the history of these châteaux. A charge is made for admission.

The purists object very strongly to flood-lighting, which casts shadows the architects never intended and emphasises details meant to be secondary. To the ordinary observer, the effect is delightful, though pretty rather than beautiful. The decoration of the châteaux is visible enough by day, but many of the present generation look at it without really seeing it until a spotlight picks it out piecemeal.

The commentary is usually well written, and spoken in the perfectly articulated French of the classical theatre. To those with a reasonable knowledge of the language it proves most interesting.

These *spectacles de son et de lumière*, 'of sound and light', have drawn great crowds and brought in much-needed money. Even those who consider them as some sort of a profanation of the night should be grateful for their introduction, for without this extra financial aid there might, in some cases, have been left only a fast-decaying building to admire by daylight.

CHRONOLOGICAL TABLE OF THE KINGS OF FRANCE

(from the thirteenth century to the Revolution)

	Came to Throne
Philippe II (Philippe-Auguste) – – – –	1180
Louis VIII – – – – – – –	1223
Louis IX (Saint Louis) – – – – –	1226
Philippe III (Philippe-le-Bel) – – – –	1285
Louis X – – – – – – – –	1314
Jean I – – – – – – – –	1316
Philippe V – – – – – – –	1316
Charles IV – – – – – – –	1322

The Valois Kings, descended from the brother of Philippe III

Philippe VI – – – – – – –	1328
Jean II – – – – – – –	1350
Charles V – – – – – – –	1364
Charles VI – – – – – – –	1380
Charles VII (Joan of Arc's 'Dauphin') – – –	1422
Louis XI – – – – – – –	1461
Charles VIII – – – – – –	1483

The Valois-Orleans King, descended from Louis d'Orléans, brother of Charles VI

Louis XII – – – – – –	1498

The Valois-Orleans Kings, descended from the third son of Louis d'Orléans

	Came to Throne
François I – – – – – – –	1515
Henri II – – – – – – – –	1547
François II (husband of Mary, Queen of Scots) –	1559
Charles IX – – – – – – –	1560
Henri III – – – – – – – –	1574

The Bourbon Kings, descended from the sixth son of Louis IX

Henri IV – – – – – – – –	1589
Louis XIII – – – – – – –	1610
Louis XIV – – – – – – –	1643
Louis XV – – – – – – –	1715
Louis XVI – – – – – – –	1774
decapitated	1793

EVENTS IN THE LIFE OF
JOAN OF ARC

(The Hundred Years War began in 1337)

Joan born in Domrémy, probably on January 6 –	1412	
Joan heard her first Voices – – May	1424	
First visit to Vaucouleurs – – – May	1428	
Second visit to Vaucouleurs January-February	1429	
Left Vaucouleurs for Chinon – February 23	1429	
Arrived at Sainte-Catherine-de-Fierbois March 4		
Arrived at Chinon – – – – March 6		
At Chinon, Poitiers, Tours and Blois March-April		
Left Blois for Orleans – – – April 25		
Entered Orleans – – – – April 29		
Siege of Orleans raised – – – May 8		
Joan left Orleans – – – – May 10		
Victory of Patay – – – – June 18		
First visit to Sully – – – – June 20 (?)		
Charles VII crowned at Rheims – – July 17		
Second visit to Sully – – – March 3-28 1430		
Joan taken prisoner – – – – May 23		
Joan's trial began – – – – January 9 1431		
Joan burnt at the stake – – – May 30		

The rehabilitation of Joan began in 1450, and was continued in 1452, 1455 and 1456. Her beatification was in 1909, and canonization in 1920.

SOME RENAISSANCE DATES

1494 François I born (died 1547)
1496 Claude de Guise born (died 1550)
1498 Jean de Guise, Cardinal de Lorraine born (died 1550)
1519 Henri II born (died 1559)
1519 François de Guise born (murdered 1563)
1519 Admiral Coligny born (murdered, Saint Bartholomew's day, 1572)
1522 Joachim du Bellay born (died 1560)
1524 Ronsard born (died 1585)
1525 Charles de Guise, Cardinal de Lorraine born (died 1574)
1544 François II born (died 1560)
1550 Charles IX born (died 1574)
1550 Henri de Guise born (assassinated 1588)
1551 Henri III born (assassinated 1589)
1553 Henri IV born (died 1610)
1553 Death of Rabelais
1589 Death of Catherine de Médicis.

Index

CHATEAUX OF THE LOIRE
R. Sarthe
Nogent-le-Rotrou
R. Huisme
Le Mans
Epuis
R. Sarthe
La Flèche
Château-du-Loir
R. Loir
R. Loir
Chateau-Renault
R. Maine
Angers
R. Loire
R. Loire
TOURS
Vouvray
Cinq-Mars-la-Pile
LANGEAIS
VILLANDRY
R. Cher
RIGNY-USSÉ
Saumur
AZAY-LE-RIDEAU
MONTSOREAU
R. Loire
CHINON
FONTEVRAULT
R. Vienne
LOCHE
R. Thouet
R. Vienne
R. Creuse